MUSEA NOSTRA

EDITED BY VALENTIN VERMEERSCH AND JEAN-MARIE DUVOSQUEL

MEMLINGMUSEUM

BRUGES

HILDE LOBELLE-CALUWE

Gemeentekrediet

BELGIAN MUNICIPAL CREDIT INSTITUTION

SUMMARY

Cover :
Hans Memling (1435/40 - 1494)
Altarpiece of St. John the Baptist and St. John the Evangelist, 1479
Detail central panel, St. Barbara.

Frontispice :
Idem. Detail central panel, St. John the Baptist.

Hans Memling (1435/40 - 1494)
Altarpiece of St. John the Baptist and St. John the Evangelist, 1479
Detail right-hand panel. St. John the Evangelist writes the book of Revelations.

The Memling Museum in the St. John's Hospital in Bruges

Gables beside the Reie.
14th century sick-ward and convent (1539).

Beam-endings (ca. 1460-70) with shield-bearing angels in the former monastery.

The roofage of the sick-wards, the tower and the monastery, seen from the courtyard.

THE MEMLING MUSEUM OWES ITS NAME to one of the most famous Brugean painters of the 'Autumn of the Middle Ages' : Hans Memling. The six masterpieces by this artist form the heart of a rich collection which is housed in the 12th century St. John's Hospital in Bruges. Various of these artworks were created in the course of time on behalf of the life of the hospital and of the hospital community itself. This accounts for the intimate link which exists here between the contents and the architecture, whereby the old hospital buildings, quite remarkable in themselves, may be regarded as one of the most typical medieval hospital complexes of Northern Europe.

The St. John's Hospital is one of the oldest charitable institutions which were founded in Bruges on the initiative of the city bourgeoisie as far back as the 12th century. It owes its name to its patron saint : St. John the Evangelist. From the start the institution was named 'domus beati Johannis' or the house of St. John. Later the other John, namely St. John the Baptist, was to keep constant company with the Evangelist, and both of them or their attributes alone, the lamb and the chalice respectively, appear on all kinds of objects and also on the hospital's coat-of-arms.

The oldest preserved document connected with St. John's dates from 1188, but archaeological traces point to the origin of a first room in about 1150. These first rules already provide much information about the function of the St. John's Hospital, about the management and about the inmates. Initially the hospital was open to virtually anybody in need. The poor, the sick and the weak found shelter here beside pilgrims and travellers, only those suspected of contagious diseases were refused entry. To begin with the medical care was very limited : only surgeons and barbers had access. University-trained doctors, officially attached to the institution, are only found from 1600 onwards. During the middle ages 'care of the soul' was deemed far more important than proper medical attention. In this way the medieval hospitals always strove to obtain the statute of a separate parish.

This was also the case here and from the 13th century onwards the domain was able to have its own priest at its disposal. In this manner there was somebody present day and night to accompany the sick on their deathbeds. At the same time the right was granted to have a churchyard and to hang two bells in the tower. It was also a rule with the medieval hospital's that the church premises should be directly accessible from the wards. Here the church is established in a part of the northern ward.

From the beginning the hospital was under the supervision of the city magistrate, who was represented until the 18th century by two guardians. Numerous works of art still testify to their management. In 1796, after the French Revolution, a separate administration was formed, which was charged with the control of the remaining charitable institutions. The Public Centre for

Jan Beerblock (1739 - 1806)
View inside the old Sick-wards, ca. 1778
Detail portraying a doctor visiting the sick with a sister. The university-trained doctor, who carried out purely intellectual work such as making a diagnosis and prescribing suitable remedies, is only found here after 1600.

Detail with man-servant who is taking away remains of food with a wheelbarrow. The person on the left is probably a surgeon. Since the middle ages it was the craft-trained surgeons and barbers who were responsible for bodily care.

9

Part of the middle sick-ward (beginning of 13th century). The stair-tower, on the western gable, leads to the monumental attic. The small window was probably used for watching over the sick-ward at night. The baroque door of 1641 was placed here in 1833. Before that it closed off the Cornelius Chapel.

Visit of the St. Ursula shrine.
Detail from the watercolour design by Flori Van Acker for the poster ,,Bruges, La ville Musée", 1911.

Small reliquary shrine of St. Ursula.
Flanders, about 1380-1400
Wood, painted, 19,5 × 28 × 14
Inv. O.SJ149.V

Social Welfare (O.C.M.W.), which still has the Memling Museum under its wing, grew out of the 18th century Commission for Civic Almshouses. The hospital staff was responsible for daily management on the spot. This hospital staff originally consisted of a community of lay brothers and sisters. The brothers were charged with the administration and with the conservation of the patrimony. The sisters were active in caring for the sick and with household work. In the second half of the 15th century they evolved into a canonical community. The community of brothers disappeared in the course of the 16th century. Various portraits of these people are preserved here, the best known of which may be seen in Hans Memling's panels.

Until 1864 the sick were housed in these old hospital buildings. The important developments in medicine in the course of the 19th century, the numerous new specialisations which were created and the technical infrastructure which they made essential, together with the realization that the patients needed to be accomodated in a more suitable manner, necessitated the building of a new hospital. The medieval wards lost their original function and, partly thanks to the numerous art

treasures which remained in them, were to be converted into a museum a century later.

Meanwhile the name of the Memling Museum had come to be known far and wide. The Memling panels have never in fact been consigned to oblivion. In the course of the centuries many a famous visitor rang at the hospital gate asking to view and admire these paintings. Interest in these unique works of art gradually increased from the beginning of the 19th century. They played an important rôle in the enthusiasm which was aroused in this period of the Romantic age for the 'Flemish Primitives'. Illustrative of this are the words of Sulpice Boisserée after a visit to the ancient hospital : 'Eine wahre Schatzkammer'. In 1839 the former 'Superior Room' in the convent was also opened to the public and one of the city's oldest museums was thus born.

The 'St. John's altar' was situated here as far back as the 17th century. The Ursula shrine was moved from the church to the museum room and the other panels were also housed here. Besides these, other paintings, sculpture and furniture were collected, insofar as there was space in the small room. During the first half of the 19th century the hospital's own collection was con-

siderably supplemented with works of art originating from the charitable institutions abolished after the French Revolution. Numerous visitors from all over Europe came to admire these art treasures. By 1845 plans had already been made to create new museum space. These were however never carried out, but another solution was in fact found. The Brugean architect Louis DelaCenserie was commissioned to rearrange the museum room so that only the six works by Hans Memling should continue to be mounted there. In April 1891 the museum with its renewed neo-baroque interior was re-opened. Some of the remaining works of art stayed behind in the old sick-wards. For the most important part of the collection new rooms were designed in the secretariat of the Civic Almshouses, 4 Kartuizerinnenstraat.

The museum of 'The Civic Almshouses' opened its doors here in 1894. In the nineteen-fifties the number of visits had so increased that the little Memling Museum could no longer afford this stream of tourists the chance to enjoy the works of art at their ease.

The medieval sick-wards were partly reorganized and a part of the southern nave was arranged so as to be

The 16th century cloister of the former monastery.

The cross-beams of the 16th century pharmacy premises.

able to house the 'Memlings'. In 1958, the year of the World Exhibition in Brussels, the famous panels were mounted here together with some of the works of art drawn from the 'Museum for Civic Almhouses' which was closed after 1945. The remaining sick-wards were also decorated, so that the visitor could now also fully enjoy the atmosphere of the medieval sick-wards.

In 1971 the hospital chemists were rehoused, so that the historic 17th century pharmacy, established in a part of the old monastery, could be added to the museum. As of now the medieval sick-wards with the church and a part of the monastery can be visited. It was not until 1976 that the O.C.M.W. management employed an art-historian responsible for the art patrimony. Partly thanks to the exhibition '800 years St. John's Hospital' in 1976 even greater interest was aroused in this important monument and its rich contents, both of which evoke centuries of hospital history. In this way a need came to be felt for reorganizing the museum and its lay-out. This reorganization will occur in the coming years in different phases. During the first phase the church, for museological and historical reasons, will be arranged as a 'Memling Museum'. It is

certainly not the intention to recreate the 'medieval situation'. The space has undergone too many drastic alterations for this. The church interior with its complete furnishings, as it has grown through the ages, will be preserved. The Memling paintings, which formed a part of the 15th century upholstery, will again be installed there. The rest of the patrimony is to be exhibited in the hospital wards. It is not an evenly built up collection offering a complete art-historical survey. They are all items made for the hospital or a selection of items deriving from other institutions, which illustrate the charitable history of the city and at the same time testify to a local artistic tradition of high quality.

The visit is organized in such a way that the sick-wards are first visited, so that the Memling Museum housed in the church is a central feature. A direct exit leads to the street. From here one continues to a separate building which houses the 17th century pharmacy and the guardians' room : the former monastery. From the first patio one obtains a splendid view of the roofs of the hospital buildings with the spire of the Church of Our Lady in the background.

The hospital domain
and the historic buildings

The entry gate to the domain.

*Detail from the city plan (1562) of Marcus Gerards with the hospital domain.
Above left in the corner are the three sick-wards with the adjoining monasteries. The churchyard chapel is also depicted.*

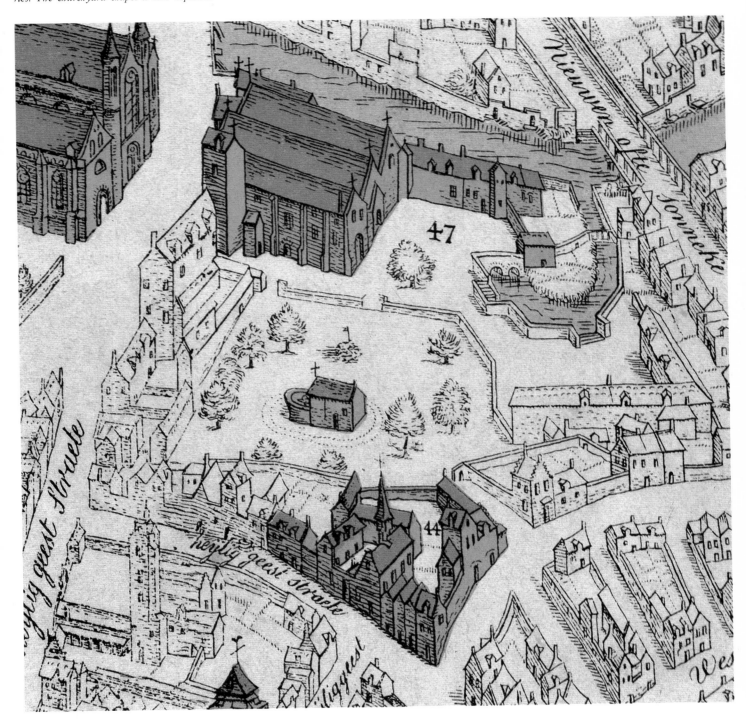

Caritate, tot het Celebren Van Missen.
Voor de geloviqe zielen, Wiens Lichaemen,
in Strooÿ begraven Sijn. Bidt voor hun.

Anonymous, 18th century
Charity-scene with view of the churchyard chapel.
Panel, oil, 65 × 40.2
Inv. O.SJ62.1

Anonymous, 1820
View of the West gables of the old sick-wards.
Canvas, oil, 32 × 41
In the foreground runs a branch of the Reie. The gate behind provides access
to the churchyard. In the 17th century a room was built against the west
gable of the northern sick-ward, in which the washing was dried. In 1820 a
kind of passage could be seen beside the central and south nave, which led to
the convent.
Inv. O.SJ63.1

The hospital domain

EVERYTHING SUGGESTS THAT THE surface of the site, since the founding of the institution in the 12th century, underwent no further alterations.

It is one of the largest domains in the city centre, lying in the midst of the Meersen. These were originally low-lying grasslands.

At the time of its foundation St. John's lay at the edge of the city, just inside the ramparts, which were then formed by the Reie. Water was of vital importance for a hospital : one arm of the Reie still flows under the sick-wards. The most important gable faced the Mariastraat, which was a busy thoroughfare of traffic towards the town centre. The oldest existing detailed description of the terrain dates from 1547 and agrees completely with what can be seen on the map which Marcus Gerards engraved in 1562. At that time the greatest part of the still existing historical buildings with the sick-wards, the monastery and the convent, had already been erected. Barns, stables, a brewery and a bakery surrounded an inner courtyard lying to the west of the sick-wards and the convent. Beside the Reie there was a large herb-garden and there was also an orchard and land under cultivation. The greater part of this enclosed garden, however, was occupied on the northern side by the churchyard. In the centre was the 15th century churchyard chapel in which the bodies of the deceased were placed upon a bier before being buried in the churchyard. Apart from the sick who died in the hospital, this was also the burial place of all those found dead in the streets of the city as well as those condemned to death. The sisters and brothers were laid to rest in the church. On an anonymous 18th century panel, *The*

HET OUD HOSPITAEL VAN St JAN IN BRUGGE 1820.

Charity Picture with View of the Churchyard Chapel, is depicted this simple single-naved chapel which disappeared in the 19th century. The painting was intended to encourage charity in the passers-by. The alms collected in this way served to provide a godly burial-service for the very poor, who were buried in straw and could not afford a coffin.

A monumental anonymous 18th century canvas, *View of the Western Gables of the old Sick-Wards,* gives a good picture of the almost countrylike atmosphere which reigned in the domain. To the left of the western gables of the three sick-wards one can see the large trees of the churchyard.

In front of the convent, to the right, there is a garden. Beside one arm of the Reie, which flowed through the inner part in a broad curve, there was a washing-platform and a drinking-place for animals. The

sick walk around outside, clothed in mantles made of red and blue linen, these being the colours of the city.

This situation remained unchanged until the middle of the 19th century. Then eight new sick-wards were erected, built round a rectangular inner courtyard. Gradually, from the end of the last century, the grounds were completely built on. Especially over the last decades this was done with little attention to planning. In 1978, when all the hospital services had left the centuries-old site, and the domain no longer served its original purpose, its appearance was quite confusing. Meanwhile a certain amount of rehabilitation work was carried out. The busy activity of recent years has disappeared and tourists come here now to enjoy peace and quiet. The accent once again falls on the historic buildings, which now finally serve the purposes of a museum.

Carrying-chair
Bruges, 18th century
Wood, painted linen, 171.5 × 66.5 × 74.5
The parochial charity organizations also possessed their own carrying-chairs
for transporting the sick. This example was the property of the poor people's
charity of St. Gillis.
Inv. O.SJ820.XXIX

Carrying-chair
Bruges, 18th century
Wood, painted, 160 × 67 × 76.5
A similar example can be seen in the painting by J. Beerblock with
View inside the old Sick-wards (ca. 1778).
The sick were brought to the hospital on carrying-chairs of this kind.
This was the property of St. John's.
Inv. O.SJ773, XXIX

Anonymous, 18th century
West gables of the old Sick-wards.
Canvas, oil, 245 × 168
Inv. O.SJ307.I

The patio garden of the pharmacy.

Two corbels, 14th century.

The historic buildings

The sick-wards and the church.

ARCHAEOLOGICAL TRACES POINT TO the fact that a first sick-ward was erected in about 1150. This was confirmed by excavations which were carried out during the winter of 1983-84. The ground plan and apearance of this first building can now be reconstructed with relative certainty. It must have been a building in the length, with a rectangular ground plan, with its long gable facing the Mariastraat. The hall, divided by supports, was probably vaulted and had a storey. An idea of the atmosphere which must have reigned here can still be obtained by visiting St. Basil's chapel on the Burg. At the beginning of the 13th century the still-existing middle hall was built, at right-angles to the first. In so doing the original garden wall was broken through. The three pointed arches in a diagonal direction on the East side make this evident.

The still-existing sick-wards form three equally wide halls with their shorter gables facing the street. This hall-type, with rectangular ground-plan, was in most common use in the building of medieval hospitals.

This provides for a large space inside, sometimes with a storey added, and the whole covered with a saddle-roof. These three halls of the 13th and 14th century completely absorbed the first sick-ward. The northern nave (end 13th century) houses the church in the front.

The three monumental sick-wards are largely built in the so-called Tournai style. The forms of the gables testify above all to the romanesque style from Tournai, which spread via the basin of the Schelde. At the time of the last two building campaigns this style was certainly striving for an archaic effect. It is not surprising therefore that the gothic form was introduced in the 14th century gable. This architecture is a typically mixed form of traditions from civic and religious building art. The gables were extensively restored at the end of the previous century under the supervision of architect Louis DelaCenserie.

Little was changed in the course of time in the volume of these halls. They still dominate the remaining buildings on the site and the houses of this quarter of the city.

The painting of 1778 by a local Brugean painter Jan Beerblock (b. 1739, d. 1806) with a *View of the Old Sick-wards*, illustrates with great feeling for pithy details life in this old hospital. The study of the numerous documents preserved in the archives allows us to conclude that the painter has created a fairly accurate picture of the interior and of hospital life as it must have gone on here for centuries. The three sick-wards and the oratory still formed one space at this time.

In 1820 the church was separated from the sick-wards. This wall spoiled for the first time the unity of the space. Later the three halls were to be further compartmentalized. After 1864 these halls would still serve in case of need. Until the beginning of this century patients were housed here from time to time.

23

The gables along the Mariastraat.

The west gables of the sick-wards.

Jan Beerblock (1739-1806)
View inside the old Sick-wards, ca. 1778.
Canvas, oil, 82 × 153. Inv. O.SJ160.I

Jan Beerblock (1739 - 1806)
View inside the old Sick-wards, ca. 1778 (details).

Detail with two men who have just brought in a sick person on a carrying-chair from the parish of St. Anna. Carrying with the 'troghe' is already mentioned in the 16th century. Carriage was free of charge.

When a sick person was admitted he had first to make confession. Afterwards his possessions were registered. Upon his decease this became the property of the hospital. Patients got a night-gown and cap from the institution.

From the beginning the sisters were responsible for housekeeping and care of the sick. The little painting with the churchyard chapel over their heads is still preserved.

Maids and man-servants help the sisters. At that time, mainly out of ignorance, no objection was taken to animals running around in the ward.

Numerous visitors have always been impressed by the standard of cleanliness in the hospital; here a sister is sweeping the passage. To the right sits a Brugean woman who is visiting a patient. It was only from 1762 that fixed visiting hours were determind. At the beginning of the 19th century these were set on Mondays and Thursdays from eight to nine o'clock.

Detail with a group of clerics, the superior and a hospital guardian.

The beds in the middle of the passages are called 'bastard beds'. They were probably used to accomodate the sick who were in need of most care. At the end of the 18th century religious accompaniment ore 'care of souls' was still very important, as appears here. At the back of the bed there are pewter utensils.

The wooden beds stood in rows along the pillars.
Each row formed a separate department with its own customs, rights and property. In the 18th century there was certainly a 'men's row', a 'women's row', a 'surgeons' row' and a 'corner for the dying'. About 100 beds were in use.

Box, 17th century
Wood, painted, 24.8 × 42 × 30
These served for the storage of resins. The 'Santalum album Citrinum et Rubrum' is white, yellow and red sandalwood. It causes transpiration.
Inv. O.SJ822.V

Small wooden barrel, 17th century
Wood, painted, h. 36.8, d. 26.5
These served for the storage of the herbs in the pharmacy. This contained Iceland Moss (Lichen Islandicus), a remedy for coughs.
Inv. O.SJ821.V

Monastery situated beside the Mariastraat with the typical romanesque tower adjoining.

The monastery with the old pharmacy and the guardians' room

NEXT TO THE TYPICAL LITTLE ROMANESQUE tower the monastery stretches out along the Mariastraat. When one enters the hospital domain by the age-old entrance-gate one obtains a good idea of the place where the brothers lived.

The long building or main building was erected at the beginning of the 14th century. At the beginning of the 16th century the premises with the small chapel were built along the side of the garden. The 'masons' signs' or house-marks in glazed brick were added by architect L. DelaCenserie during restoration works at the beginning of this century. The houses which border the premises to the East date from the 16th and 14th centuries. The last of these houses on the first floor the legendary 'Memling room' where Hans Memling is said to have painted the St. Ursula shrine. The master, who was superintendant of the hospital, lived in this room. The atmospheric and simple cloister has a typically assymetrical roofage which surrounds an intimate little inner courtyard. On the ground floor was the refectory with a kitchen in the adjoining house. On the first floor the attic was arranged as a dormitory and the adjoining rooms were used by the administration.

In December 1643 it was decided to install a pharmacy in the previous monastery. This hospital pharmacy remained in use until 1971 and was then made into a museum. In 1643 a pharmacist, member of the 'Neerynghe van de Cruydhalle', was engaged to arrange the room and for about ten years he gave instruction to two sisters who took over his duties in 1655.

The painting by Philippe Van Bree, *View of the Pharmacy of the St. John's Hospital* (first half 19th century), shows the hospital pharmacy in full activity. The presence of the young mother with her typical Brugean cape and bonnet, holding her sick son in her lap, suggests that out-patients were also treated here. There are four highly active sisters. To the right sits a nun sorting herbs with the still-preserved herb-book of Dodoens at her feet. A second sister is pounding raw materials in the large bronze mortar. Behind the dispensing table the woman pharmacists are preparing the medicines. The nun behind the baroque table is sister Francisca van Becelaere. The interior is little changed. One still finds a homely atmosphere there, which the painter has suggested so well with the sunlight coming in warmly and the sleeping cat on the foot-rest.

The furnishing dates largely from the 17th and 18th centuries. In the course of the latter century the pharmacy and the adjoining drawing-room acquired their present 18th century appearance with doors and ceiling decorations in Louis XV style. All the furnishings and recipients necessary for the good functioning of a pharmacy are present here. Central is the imposing 17th century oak *dispensing-table* with simple but typical early baroque framework and carving. The numerous drawers on the front side might also suggest the treatment of out-patients. In the drawers of the simple 18th century *herb-chest* the dried herbs were kept. The *plaster-chest* was accomodated in a niche in the wall. It is protected by a door of glass in lead. This chest was intended for preserving very precious remedies, namely the plasters. These plasters have played a very important part in medicine from olden times right up to the beginning of this century. The plasters consisted of salves which were spread out on textiles and kept rolled up in the various compartments. On each compartment the name is painted. Sometimes venerable names, which demonstrate how much respect the ancient medical art had for these remedies : e.g. E. Gracia : the plaster of

Philippe Van Bree, first half 19th century
View inside the old Pharmacy of the St. John's Hospital.
Panel, oil, 90 × 110
Inv. O.SJ.79.I

View inside the old Pharmacy with the 17th century dispensing table.

God's grace, used in order to dry wounds ; or E. Divinum, named the Divine plaster, against corns.

The numerous little *boxes* in which dried resins and gums were kept, used for making the plasters, suggest that this preparation occured on the premises. The 18th century oak chest beside the plaster-chest has full door-panels with two little drop-doors in the middle. The little compartments inside and the labels on the edges point to the fact that this was the *poison-chest*. It had to be possible to close this completely. The small 18th century chest above the oblong piece of furniture in the middle of the shelves is the *simples-chest*. In a simples-chest a sample was kept of most raw materials or simplicia, such as herbs, resins and minerals with preparations or composita were made.

The small chest has 8 cardboard drawers with samples arranged in the compartments. Two drawers can be seen on the dispensing-table. They were used for training the women pharmacists and as reference.

The *mortars* were not used exclusively in pharmacies but also in housework, e.g. in the kitchen. The raw materials were pulverized by means of a metal pestle. Examples in bronze, stone, marble and porcelain can be

The plaster chest in the 17th century pharmacy with (right) the poison chest.

The guardians' room.

The pharmacy with the simple chest.
On the shelves 17th century jugs, chemists' pots and 19th century bottles.

seen here. On the shelves stand *pharmacists' pots and other recipients*. The oldest pots are the series of brown gravelstone bearded jars purchased in the 17th century. Medicinal waters, wines and syrups were preserved in these. Later a series of pharmacists' pots was ordered in white glazed clay with a blue label. They were made after 17th century models. In the cartouche with the well-known peacock motif and angel's head underneath the name of the preparation is written in each case. The form determines the content. In the bottles closed with a wooden stopper 'herbal waters' were usually kept. The A(qua) on the label points to this. The cylindrical pots, mostly with 19th century pewter lids, contain salves : U(nguentum), pills : P(ilulae) and extracts Ex(tractum). The cylindrical examples with nozzles served as oil-pots : O(leum). The syrup-pots : S(irupus) have a foot and a nozzle with a wooden stopper. These are also closed with 19th century pewter lids, mostly made in Bruges. From the 19th century onwards the clay recipients were replaced by glass bottles with domes, provided with various kinds of labels. Small cylindrical pots are still to be found on the shelves, turned from one piece of wood and supplied with a lid, and used for conserving all kinds of raw materials. At the top still stand little barrels and 17th century boxes. They are all painted in imitation mahogany with gilded

titles designating on the one hand the names of vegetable medicines such as liquorice-roots and poppy-heads, and on the other hand the resins which were stored in them.

The adjoining room was formerly called the drawing-room of the pharmacy. With its baroque oak furniture it still has the atmosphere of a cosy Flemish drawing-room. Since 1891, with the rearrangement of the Memling Museum, two series of guardians' portraits were housed here, so that this room gradually came to be known as the 'Guardians' Room'. One series, with explanatory text underneath, shows the directors of St. John's. The other series shows the guardians of St. Julian's, the former hospital for 'Backward people and foundlings'. A series of so-called 'Delft' tiles (17th century) decorates the wall. They represent all kinds of games.

The convent of the sisters

THE CONVENT, WHICH STRETCHES along the Reie behind the southern sick-ward, was built in the 16th and 17th centuries. Since it is still lived in by some of the hospital sisters, these premises are not open to the public.

The paintings of Hans Memling

Diptych with the Virgin and Martin van Nieuwenhove, 1487.
*Detail of the left-hand panel. One of Memling's
best known Madonna figures.*

Altarpiece of St. John the Baptist and St. John the
Evangelist, 1479.
*Central panel. On the frame appears the text
'Opus Johannis Memling' and the date
'MCCCCLXXIX - 1479'.*

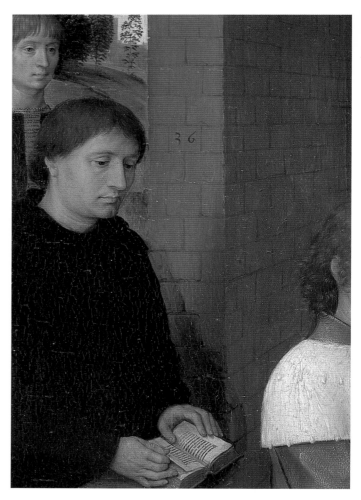

Triptych with the Lamentation over Christ, 1480.
Detail from the left-hand panel. The donor, a hospital brother, is Adriaan Reins, who died in 1490.

Triptych with the Adoration of the Magi, 1479.
Detail of the central panel with the donor brother Jan Floreins at the age of 36.

THE MOST RENOWNED PAINTINGS OF the collection, which draw tens of thousands of visitors to this old hospital every year, are unquestionably the six masterpieces by Hans Memling. Four of these panels were made for St. John's. The two others from the St. Julian's Hospice were brought here after the French Revolution. Hans Memling may be considered as one of the most important later figures among the group of painters who are designated in art history under the name 'Flemish Primitives'.

They were active during the greater part of the 15th century and they dominated and made great the art of painting to the North of the Alps. One of the most famous founders of this school is Jan Van Eyck (b. ca. 1390-d. 1441). The name 'Flemish' should however be interpreted in a broader sense. It was not only the important Flemish trade centres such as Ghent and Bruges which played a part, but substantial works were

also produced in other areas of the Burgundian territory such as Holland, Hainault and Brabant. Most artists were also not of Flemish origin, but came to settle in the cities where the Burgundian court resided or where foreign merchants lived who could act as a Maecenas. This was certainly the case in Bruges. A new mentality lay at the basis of the important innovations which they introduced : an interest in the visible and tangible world and in man, who occupies an important place in this world. These new conceptions, with a humanistic undertone, can be considered as a northern forerunner to the renaissance. The stream of ideas was similar to that which existed in Italy, where it gave birth to 15th century art, characterized as early renaissance. In our part of the world, in the 15th century, these new attainments are to be found above all in the art of painting. The new style grew out of the 'International Style'. A courtly art, in which an unreal, ideal and extremely refined, scarcely realistic and problem-free world was

Altarpiece of St. John the Baptist and St. John the Evangelist, 1479.
The figures of the donors on the left-hand outside panel are two hospital brothers : Jacob de Keuninc and Antheunis Seghers.

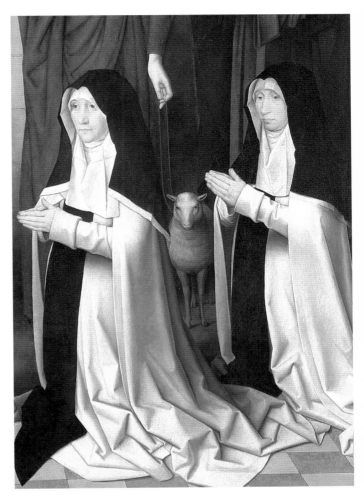

Altarpiece of St. John the Baptist and St. John the Evangelist, 1479.
The figures of the donors on the back of the right-hand panel are two hospital sisters : Agnes Casembrood and Clara van Hulsen.

depicted in a splendour of form and colour. The new realizations must have created a shock effect. The artists tried to depict reality. The panel is like an open window with a view into a three-dimensional world, characterized by depth and continuity and by the same surroundings in which men live and move.

An effort is made to paint people and objects true to nature. Attention is paid to the forms themselves, to the materials and to the tangible rendering of their surface. In an empirical way a logical perspective effect is striven for. Special use is made of 'atmospheric perspective', that is to say that in reality the air acts as a kind of screen which makes the outlines of the most distant objects less defined, so that they lose colour intensity. The light also plays an important rôle, it gives form and colour. The use of a technique lies at the basis of these qualitatively remarkable realizations. Although oil paint had already been used for painting on other materials,

these artists employed this medium for the first time in the art of panel-painting. This permitted enormous colour variations and the possibility of imitating the density and surface of all kinds of materials.

This new realistic art manifested itself in about 1420. One of the major figures in the early period is Jan Van Eyck. An all-embracing personality who can be considered not only as a craftsman, but also as court painter to Duke Philip the Good, for whom he even carried out diplomatic missions. Van Eyck settled finally in Bruges in 1430 and died there in 1441. His work bears witness to an exceptional analytic spirit which observes every object with equal interest and reflects reality in the smallest details. He discovers reality and makes it visible with light and colour. For the first time he makes use of atmospheric perspective and applies in a consequent manner the entry of light, the play of light and the reflection of light.

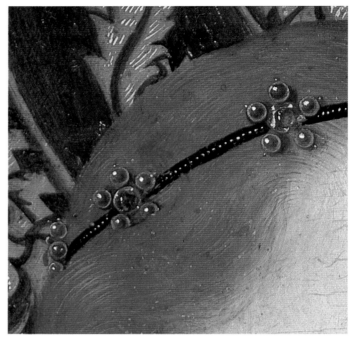

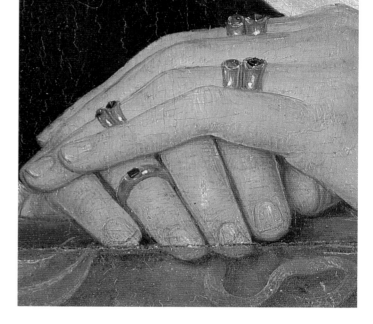

Altarpiece of St. John the Baptist and St. John the Evangelist, 1479.
Detail of the central panel. The golden crown of St. Catharine studded with precious stones and pearls.

Portrait of a Woman, 1480.
Detail. The little cross on the golden neck-chain consists of precious stones in small golden boxes, from which three pearls hang.

Altarpiece of St. John the Baptist and St. John the Evangelist, 1479.
Detail from the central panel. The ribbon round the Virgin's head is adorned with jewels.

Portrait of a Woman, 1480.
Detail. The fingers adorned with seven gold rings rest on the frame, which creates the illusion that the person is looking out of a window.

Diptych with the Virgin and Martin van Nieuwenhove, 1487.
Detail of right-hand panel. Here too the materials are portrayed with great attention : the open book with gilt and decorated cut, the velvet of the sleeve tied with laces and the fur which lines the coat.

Diptych with the Virgin and Martin van Nieuwenhove, 1487.
Detail from the left-hand panel. The Virgin is holding the apple. This means that she is the 'new Eve'. The child will redeem mankind from original sin.

Altarpiece of St. John the Baptist and St. John the Evangelist, 1479.
Detail from the left-hand panel. A fine example of observation and imitation of materials.

Altarpiece of St. John the Baptist and St. John the Evangelist, 1479.
Detail of the left-hand panel with the head of John the Baptist on the dish.

Triptych with the Adoration of the Magi, 1479.
Central panel.

Altarpiece of St. John the Baptist and St. John the Evangelist, 1479.
Detail from the left-hand panel with the 'Baptism in the Jordan'. Memling paid special attention to landscape and used elements of it, such as rivers and roads, to create depth.

The St. Ursula Shrine, before 1489.
Detail of the short side with St. Ursula.

The materials represented such as textiles', fur, carpets and precious stones are almost tangible. His work testifies to a belief in the visible world in which we live. In the middle of the 15th century Rogier van der Weyden (b. 1399 - d. 1464) was to play an important rôle. Born in Tournai, where he was a student of the Master of Flémalle, he settled finally in Brussels. Rogier van der Weyden was to observe reality and isolate elements from it. He goes to work like an intellectual and an ascetic. He was to 'discover' compositions and create new types. His figures resemble coloured statues which are often barely integrated in their surroundings. The background usually seems to have been added. The attention goes entirely to the ephemeral personalities and to their expressions and the angular forms of the drapery, which all bear witness to an intensely dramatic experience, often supported by a religious feeling.

In about 1450 the master was to make a journey to Italy. He assimilated motifs from this art but they were to have no fundamental influence on his work. Bearing in mind the great influence which Rogier exercised on Memling's work, it is generally assumed that Memling worked in the atelier of the Brussels master after his return from Italy until his death in 1464. Memling was born in Seligenstadt near Frankfurt in about 1435-40. In spite of his German origin he can be considered as an exponent of the late 15th century Flemish panel-painting art. His name is always associated with Bruges. It is possible that, before he came to Brussels, he had contact with the school of Cologne. Certain stylistic attributes, especially as far as the use of colour is concerned, point to this.

In 1465 we find Memling mentioned for the first time in the books of the 'poorters' of Bruges, which implies that he was living in this city and was allowed to practice his profession here. He seems to have prospered here, for in 1480 he was accounted among the small group of the richest people in Bruges. He married Anna de Valkenaere and lived with his wife and three children in the St. Jorisstraat. Memling died in Bruges on 11th August 1494 and was buried in the Church of St. Giles.

The question may be asked why he came to settle in this city. Was it the presence of the Burgundian court, which often resided in Bruges, that attracted him ? Did he see possible patrons in the wealthy local bourgeoisie or in the foreign colony which was established here ? Definite proof that Memling, like many other painters, also worked for the Dukes of Burgundy cannot be found, but it cannot be excluded. He certainly fulfilled various commissions for members of the court. That

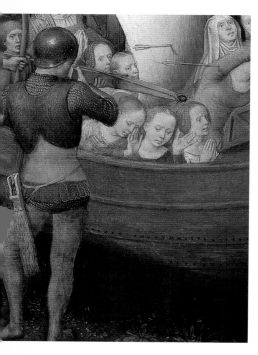

The St. Ursula Shrine.
Detail from the martyrdom scene. The soldier wears the clothing of a warrior such as could be seen in our regions in the second half of the 15th century.

The Ursula Shrine.
Detail of the long side from the portrayal of the martyrdom. Urusla rejects the marriage offer. The scene is reflected in the warrior's armour.

The Ursula Shrine.
Detail of the long side from the martyrdom scene. The executioner Dschem, brother of Sultan Bajazet II, holds the bow taut.

Memling found patrons in Bruges among the local bourgeoisie and among the members of the foreign colonies, especially the Italian, is beyond doubt.

Apart from a number of large works with religious subjects where they appear as patrons, about 25 portraits of these wealthy persons have been preserved. A respectable number which puts in the shade the remaining production of contemporaries, at least as far as this type of painting is concerned.

We also find similar examples in this collection, namely *The Portrait of a Woman or the Sibylla Sambetha* of 1480 and the portrait of *Maarten van Nieuwenhove* of 1487. Among these Brugean patrons a very special group can be distinguished, namely the brothers and sisters of the St. John's Hospital who placed four orders with Hans Memling between 1475 and 1489. Many questions concerning these orders remain unanswered.

A romantic legend originating in the 17th century and spiced with many pithy details in the 18th and 19th centuries tells that Memling joined up as a mercenary in the army of Charles the Bold, when he went to war in an attempt to unite the lands of hither and thither. When the duke was killed at Nancy in 1477, Memling returned home and fell exhausted and sick to death before the entrance gate of the St. John's Hospital. He is said to have stayed there as a patient and to have painted the *St. Ursula shrine* in the 'Memling Room' in gratitude for his healing.

This pious legend, which persisted obstinately, inspired a number of romantic painters. Although the truth certainly lies elsewhere, the story once again shows that the Memling - St. John's Hospital link has raised many questions and has certainly appealed to the imagination. The legend was dispelled by the data which the archives brought to light and which were largely found and published by the well-known English Scholar James H. Weale.

It still remains unclear, though, what relationship the painter had with the hospital, especially since he produced four masterpieces for the house, which is quite an appreciable number. Neither contracts nor payments are to be found in the archives. It should be added that during the second half of the 15th century the hospital often had to cope with financial difficulties. Disputes with the city magistrates, the governors of the institution, were the order of the day.

In order to withdraw partly from the authority of the city magistrate, they formed with the support of the bishop since 1459 a canonical community, where previously they had been a lay community, bound only by internal regulations. In this way the bishop also established his authority in this institution, where previously he had no say. This authority was however limited to religious matters. The city magistrates kept the management in their hands.

Was it in order to show greater independence from the management or to demonstrate their new status that

The St. Ursula Shrine.
Detail of the sloping roof. The central medallion which here too is considered to be atelier work represents the Coronation of the Virgin.

The Ursula Shrine.
Detail of the sloping roof. The central medallion represents Ursula and the 11,000 Virgins.

the brothers and sisters had their portraits painted in a spirit of surrender and piety ? It is also a fact that during the same period the hospital church was completely refurnished.

The large *Altarpiece of St. John the Baptist and St. John the Evangelist* was certainly ordered for the high altar and the *St. Ursula Shrine* was given a place of honour here in 1489. Although many questions remain unanswered. This ensemble is important and certainly also representative of Memling's work.

The St. John's Hospital has played a major part in keeping alive the interest in Memling's art. Early on the painter had become a figure of interest, thanks to the German Romantics, who found in his creations the reflection of a lost golden age which they situated in the late middle ages. They saw him as a Fra Angelico of the north. This success was probably responsible for the fact that Memling's work was studied long before that of the other 'Flemish Primitives'. A number of interesting points of departure for art-historical study can also be found here, since various panels are dated and bear his name. Apart from monumental work some smaller miniaturesque paintings can be seen here. The subjects, with the exception of the *Portrait of a Woman*, are of religious inspiration, which is quite normal for the period. The link with the St. John's Hospital is clear. The patron saints are often depicted, but various hospital brothers and sisters are also portrayed.

The influence of Rogier van der Weyden can be traced here in nearly every panel. Memling borrows mainly compositions, types and poses from his teacher. This phenomenon has called forth some less favourable appreciations from modern art critics, who are mainly concerned with a history of remarkable innovations.
The first discordant sounds were expressed by Friedländer in about in 1928. He claimed that the painter was neither a 'pioneer', such as Jan Van Eyck, nor a 'discoverer' such as van der Weyden. He lacks passion and for this reference is always made to the copied scenes which in Memling's case are short of dramatic power. It would however be exaggerated to interpret this phenomenon as the result of copying. Together with the observation that the painter also often reproduces his own figures, we are forced to conclude that all this forms precisely a part of the unique nature of his style. The underlying drawings prove that he always, almost restlessly sought to integrate his figures correctly in space. He also seeks, with clearly discernible artistry, to arouse the illusion of reality. He always attempts to attain a correct drawing of perspective. This 'struggle' with pencil, brush and paint had to end in a result which brings a serene and balanced picture of the world before the eyes. A mystical ideal, expressed by means of a static and contemplative art. When one examines his works very closely this conclusion is further accentuated. At first sight Memling introduces no staggering innovations. His work is rather a beautiful synthesis of what his predecessors

45

The St. Ursula Shrine, before 1489.
Detail from the 'Disembarkment in Cologne'. The St. Martin's Tower and the choir of the Cathedral are visible. One of the western towers is being built. In Memling's panels one often finds details with iconographic data about cities.

Triptych with the Lamentation over Christ, 1480.
Detail of the right-hand panel with St. Barbara.

Altarpiece of St. John the Baptist and St. John the Evangelist, 1479.
Detail of the cloth-of-honour. The metal of the Virgin's crown, the gold brocade and the velvet are almost touchable.

achieved. He does not follow the analytical vision of Jan Van Eyck to the extreme but shares its humanist vision and expresses this in the feeling for balance and in the attention to the reproduction of materials, light and colour. From Rogier he borrows mainly the formal. He softens the dramatic tensions and contradictions, however, into a conscious search for the purification of forms and the creation of rest. He tries to obtain greater legibility by creating a balanced composition. In so doing he always attemps to integrate the figures in space. This space, whether interior or landscape, he seeks to organize as reasonably as possible. To this end he certainly uses the techniques of 'atmospheric perspective' but he was also familiar with the theoretical principles of 'linear perspective'. Various traces indicate this. A stylistic immobilism characterizes his whole work.

Towards the end of his life he develops an interest in new decorative elements, primarily from the Lombardian repertoire. He must therefore have been accessible to the creations of Italian art of the pre-renaissance. With all these considerations in mind, Memling cannot be branded as a slavish imitator. His perfect style and his longing for harmony rather make one think of an early form of classicism, of first expressions of academism. This style can also be recognized in the portraits. His people are not individualized in the extreme. With the aid of a smooth technique he creates purified forms and thus obtains ideallized people. He brings innovation to the art of portrait painting. He no longer sets the patron against a neutral, dark background, but places him in a well-lit interior or against a colourful landscape.

His easily recognizable style made it quickly possible to compile a catalogue of his paintings (c. 1900) to which little has been changed. More than a hundred works have been grouped around him, which is a remarkable number. Memling's style was to make a school in Bruges and influence several painters until late in the 16th century.

Altarpiece of St. John the Baptist and St. John the Evangelist, 1479.
*Oak, oil, 176.2 × 79 (left-hand panel), 173.7 × 173.8 (centre),
176.1 × 79.2 (right-hand panel).
Inv. O.SJ175.1*

The '*Altarpiece of St. John the Baptist and St. John
the Evangelist*' (1479) must have been ordered for the
high altar. On the frame appears the name of Hans
Memling and the date 1479. The presence of St. John
the Evangelist and of St. John the Baptist in the middle
panel strengthens this supposition, since the high altar
of an oratory is generally dedicated to the patron saint.
The Evangelist holds the chalice in his hand with the
poisonous snake. An allusion to the fact that an attempt
was made to poison him. The Baptist can be recognized
by the lamb. He is wearing the camel-hair robe and is
pointing to something. This posture is based on the
gospel text where the Baptist announces the coming of
Christ with the words : 'Ecce Agnus Dei', 'Behold the
Lamb of God'. Together with two female saints they
surround the enthroned madonna. The Virgin is seated
centrally in front of a brocade cloth of honour and
under a red velvet canopy. Two angels hold a golden
crown over her head. The triangular composition of the

three seated figures in the foreground forms the basis of
the strictly symmetrical composition.
The infant Jesus on the Virgin Mary's lap is placing a
ring on St. Catherine's finger. That is why this triptych
is also often called 'The Mystic Marriage of St. Catherine'. This refers to Catherine of Sienna. The sword and
the broken wheel are the attributes of Catherine of Ale-
xandria. The reading saint, recognizable by the tower,
is Barbara. The two little angels keep the saints company. The one on the left is playing the positive or
portable organ, the one on the right is holding a book
open, whose pages the Virgin is turning. The presence
of all these holy personages round the madonna figure
suggests the theme of a 'Sacra Conversazione'. This
theme is much to Memling's taste since it enables him to
build up a highly balanced scene. The St. John figures
may be considered as the most important depictions,
seeing the attention which is paid in making their life
stories clear to the spectator with the help of many

Outer panels with the donors. Oak, oil, 176.1 × 79 (per panel).

details. On the capitals of the pillars, in the landscape and on the side-panels are depicted numerous scenes which illustrate important moments in their careers. Behind the pillars which form the vertical element in the field of composition and also limit the foreground, a landscape stretches out. The different scenes on the left in the background recount the life and martyrdom of John the Baptist. The two first episodes from the cycle are to be seen on the capitals over his head : 'The angel appears to Zacharias' to announce to him the birth of a son and the scene of 'The birth' itself. The story continues spread in zig-zag over the middle-panel and in the left-hand panel. One can see 'The preaching in the desert', 'John captured and led away' and 'The Baptist's body burned at the command of Julian the Apostate'. On the left-hand panel behind comes 'The baptism in the Jordan' and on the bank 'the Baptist points Christ out to Andrew and St. John'. To the left in the interior Salome dances for Herod. As a reward for her dance she will ask for the Baptist's head. The foreground is entirely taken up with the depiction of the martyrdom. The executioner places the head on the dish which is held by a barely alarmed Salome. Some spectators form a circle. The two personages in the foreground are inspired by the same scene in Rogier van der Weyden's St. John's altar (Staatliche Museen, Berlin).

To the right the life of the Evangelist is illustrated according to the same principle. On one capital appears 'The raising of Drusiana' and on the other 'John drinks the poisoned cup'. In the background 'the apostle is plunged in burning oil'. One can also make out how he 'baptizes the philisopher Crato' and to the far right how he is led to a little boat in which he is 'brought to the island of Patmos'. The right-hand panel is occupied completely by the vision of the Apocalypse. Seated on a circular rock in the midst of the Aegaean Sea, the Evangelist writes down the Revelation of the end of the world, which is portrayed above left. The scene enacted

in the higher spheres is shown by a rainbow. The other events will be accomplished on earth at the end of time. The most important figure in this happening is the 'Unnamed', the figure of God on the throne. In his hand he holds a sceptre and on his lap lies the book with the seven seals. The lamb jumps up and when it breaks the seals cataclysms will ravage the earth. Round the throne sit the 'Living', represented as the symbols of the evangelists : the winged lion (Mark), the winged ox (Luke), the human figure (Matthew) and the eagle (John). 'The Elders' in the outer circle sit on folding liturgical chairs. They play various instruments. Underneath stands an angel. Another angel kneels at his feet in front of the incense-altar. On the earth the most noticeable figures are the 'four horsemen of the apocalypse'. The rider on the black horse is interpreted as starvation, while 'death' on the dun horse is seen as the plague. He is pursued by the monster of hell. People

flee from them into caves. Over 'the monster of hell' fire mixed with hailstones falls onto an island. Beside this the burning piece of rock destroys ships. To the right is depicted 'the plague of giant locusts', and 'horses belching fire storm the beach'. 'The mighty angel' with fiery legs reaches up to a rainbow with his head. Above him in a medallion is 'the apocalyptic woman' encircled by the sun, with the sickle moon at her feet. A seven-headed dragon tries to take the child away.

Altarpiece of St. John the Baptist and St. John the Evangelist.
Detail of the central panel with St. Catharine. According to some authors this is a portrait of Maria of Burgundy.

Detail with the Madonna.

Detail from the central panel with St. Barbara. Behind her stands the tower with three openings, her attribute. Some authors claim that this could be a portrait of Margaret of York.

Altarpiece of St. John the Baptist and St. John the Evangelist.
Details of the central panel.
This crane stood on the Kraanplaats in Brugge. The 'crane children' are running in the wheel. A hospital brother is gauging the wine-casks from Bordeaux. Wine-measuring was a civic privilege granted to St. John's in the 14th century.

Sint John the Evangelist is plunged in boiling oil. In the background he steps into the boat which brings him to the island of Patmos, to which he was exiled.

According to some authors this is a self-portrait of Memling. The clothing, however, suggests that it is the figure of a brother.

Detail with St. John the Evangelist, the oldest patron of the hospital.

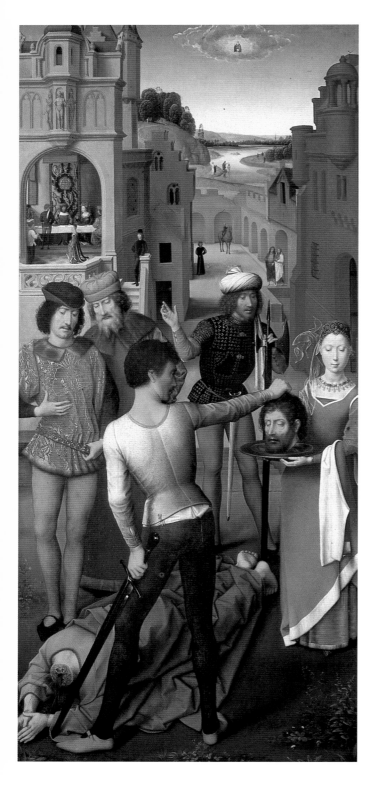

Altarpiece of St. John the Baptist and St. John the Evangelist. *Left-hand panel with the Martyrdom of John the Baptist.*

Right-hand panel with the Apocalypse.

Detail of the Apocalypse : the burning rocks which destroy the ships, the plague of grasshoppers, the fiery horses on the beach, the angel, the 'apocalyptic' woman and the seven-headed dragon.

Altarpiece of St. John the Baptist and St. John the Evangelist.
Detail of the right-hand panel with one of the horsemen of the Apocalypse.

Altarpiece of St. John the Baptist and St. John the Evangelist.
Detail of the second horseman.

Memling brings this dramatic event before our eyes with a rich range of colours. The reflection of elements in the water betrays his interest in the analysis of natural phenomena. The little figures getting smaller towards the background point to the application of 'linear perspective'. An interesting detail on the middle panel should also be mentioned, at the top and to the right of the cloth of honour. It is a view of the Kraanplaats where the wooden crane was mounted. This scene refers to a piece of hospital history. Here the barrels of Bordeaux wine were discharged from the ships. One can observe the little figures of the brothers who are measuring. The use of the measuring-rod was a civic function for measuring and gauging the arriving wine. This function was granted to the hospital in about 1300 and for centuries it represented an important source of income.

On the back panels one can see the portraits of the kneeling donors accompanied by their patron saints. They are shown standing in shallow niches. They have

Altarpiece of St. John the Baptist and St. John the Evangelist.
Detail of the horseman of the Apocalypse who symbolizes starvation.

Altarpiece of St. John the Baptist and St. John the Evangelist.
Detail from the Apocalypse. Death, on horseback, symbolizes the plague.

all been identified. From left to right one can see Jacob de Keuninc together with St. James of Compostella, clothed as a pilgrim. Abbot Anthony, recognizable by his staff and the little pig, is the patron saint of Antonius Seghers, master of the hospital. Agnes Casembrood kneels in front of St. Agnes, distinguishable by the little lamb. Finally St. Clara is holding the monstrance in her hands. In front of her is sister Clara Van Hulsen. When, on Sundays and festivals or during church services, the triptych was opened, the sick people saw this group of holy, ideallized figures motionless and in a restful atmosphere free from passion. A world containing a promise of the hereafter, where those who had suffered most on this earth would be rewarded.

The triptych was probably commissioned before 1475, since Antonius Seghers died in that year. It was placed on the high altar in 1479. It was removed from the church in the 17th century to make space in 1637 for the baroque altar.

Altarpiece of St. John the Baptist and St. John the Evangelist.
Detail of the left-hand panel. Salome dances for Herod. The scene in fact gives a picture of a meal in a late-gothic interior. On the dresser to the left stand magnificent goblets. The musicians are playing shawms and an S-shaped trumpet.

58

Altarpiece of St. John the Baptist and St. John the Evangelist.
Detail from the Apocalypse on the right-hand panel.

Pag. 61.
Triptych with the Adoration of the Magi, 1479.
*Panel, oil, 77.5 (total height), 57.2 × 46.5 (centre),
48 × 24.7 (lateral panels).
Open. The following inscriptions appear on the
frames: 'Dit werck dede maken broeder Jan
Floreins alias Vander Rijst. Broeder profess vande
hospitale van Sint Jans in Brugghe. anno
MCCCCLXXIX - Opus Johanis Memling'.
Inv. O.SJ173.I*

*Closed. The sculpture on the porticos represents
(on the left) Adam and Eve. On the right the
angel is driving them out of the earthly paradise.
On the left one sees John the Baptist, on the right
Veronica. The initials IF appear three times on the
frame.*

*Detail of the reverse side with the 15th century
iron clasps.*

Jan Floreins, brother of the hospital, was the 36-year old donor of the *Triptych with the Adoration of the Magi* (1479). His name also appears on the original frame next to the painter's name and the date. With *The Birth of Christ* and *The Dedication in the Temple* to be seen on the side-panels, these scenes are classic portraits from the cycle of Christ's youth. In all these compositions Memling has turned to Rogier van der Weyden for practical advice.

The theme of 'The Nativity' on the left-hand panel is derived from Rogier's 'Nativity' on the middle panel of the Bladelin altar (Staatliche Museen, Berlin). On the middle panel the Virgin is seated centrally in a delapidated stable. In the background a medieval city is evoked. The figures are placed around her with great feeling for balance. The oldest king kneels and kisses the Child's feet. Behind him to the right the black king steps into the stable. In front to the left the middle-aged Mage presents a vase of precious metalwork. The composition can be compared with the Adoration on van der Weyden's Columba altar (Alte Pinakotheek, Munich), The donor, Jan Floreins, kneels in an attitude of prayer behind a wall. He was master of the hospital from 1488 to 1497 and was always a controversial figure. He was the only hospital brother who survived the plague epidemic. The employment of unsuitable staff led to various difficulties. It was probably as a

result of this that he was dismissed from his post as master. He stayed on here as a brother until his death in 1504 or 1505.

On the right-hand panel is enacted the dedication in the temple. The Virgin gives the Child to Simeon. Between them stands the prophetess Anne. Joseph, a little in the background, produces turtle-doves from a small basket, this being the gift of the poor.

On the reverse side there are some splendid samples of illusionism. The frames, which form the boundary between the world of the spectator and the world of the painting, imitate marble stones. The initials of Jan Floreins appear three times, intertwined with an elegant bow. The authentic lock is a fine example of medieval wrought iron. The way in which the porticos are painted, the cut of the hearthstones, the play of light on the architecture, all lead the spectator's gaze unconsciously towards the depth, through the delicately painted landscape. To the left sits John the Baptist, to the right Veronica. Similar porticos can also be found by his Brussels teacher. The nuances of colour here are remarkable. This triptych bears resemblances to Memling's triptych preserved in Madrid (Prado) which dates from a few years earlier. Here, however, the composition is built up in a much more balanced way.

Triptych with the Adoration of the Magi, 1479.
Detail from the left-hand panel with the Virgin kneeling before the Infant Christ. St. Joseph, in the background, holds a burning candle which implies that the 'Divine Light' is present.

Detail from the central panel. This portrayal of one of the kings is considered by some authors to be a portrait of duke Charles the Bold.

Detail of the right-hand outer panel with Veronica.

Detail from the central panel. Behind the Virgin a medieval city is depicted.

Triptych with the Lamentation over Christ, 1480.
Panel, oil, 44 × 14 (lateral panels), 44 × 36 (centre).
Inv. O.SJ177.I

Outer panels with left St. Wilgeforte and right Mary of Egypt incorporated in
the architecture in an illusionist way.

Brother Adriaan Reins commissioned the smallest triptych with *The Lamentation over Christ* (1480). He kneels in the company of his patron saint, St. Adrian, in the left-hand panel. A landscape in which the typical woods betray the hand of the painter serves as background for the three panels. The lamentation, in the centre is far less dramatic than Rogier Van der Weyden's composition which served as model (Mauritshuis, The Hague). The figure of St. John even comes across somewhat woodenly and could be the work of a pupil.

The refined and elegant female saints have been fitted into the small side-panels with a fine sense of proportion so as to create an illusion. The variety and delicate tone gradations of colour and the detailed painting of plants make this little triptych a priceless gem.

Triptych with the Lamentation over Christ.
Detail of the back of the left-hand panel. Wilgeforte is portrayed with beard and cross. This legendary saint wished to remain a virgin and only become the bride of Christ. Her suitor was deterred because she had grown a beard. Her father had her crucified for this. In Flanders she was appealed to in order to be delivered from all distress.

Detail of the back of the right-hand panel. Mary of Egypt, the naked sinner, retired into the desert to repent. The three loaves she took with her kept her alive for forty years.

The St. Ursula Shrine, before 1489.
Wood, gilt and painted, 87 × 33 × 91
Inv. O.SJ176.I

Pages 68 - 69.
Short side with the Virgin and figures of two donors. These hospital sisters have been identified as Jossine van Dudzeele and Anna van den Moortele.

Short side with St. Ursula who protects ten Virgins with her mantle. In her hand she holds her attribute, the arrow with which she was martyred.

Pages 70 - 71.
Gilt and polychromed corner statuettes : St. John the Evangelist, St. Agnes, St. Elizabeth, St. James.

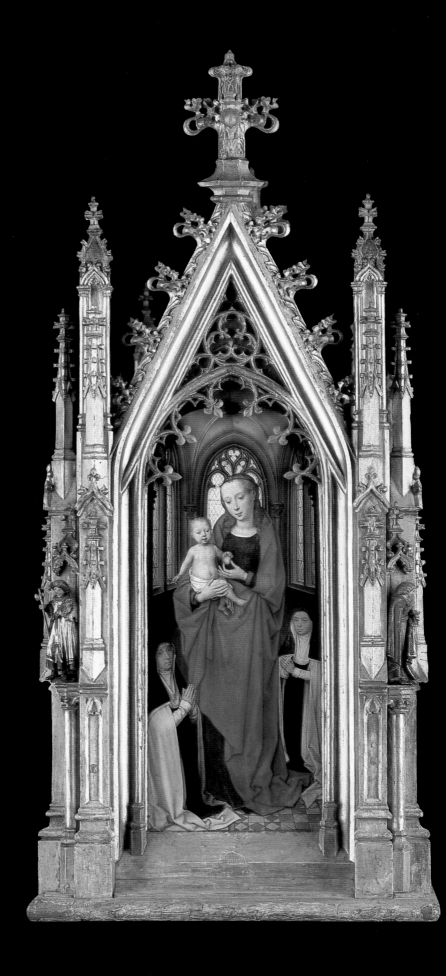

The St. Ursula Shrine.
Detail from the sloping roof with an angel playing a psaltery.

The St. Ursula Shrine.
Detail from the sloping roof with an angel playing a viol.

The St. Ursula Shrine (before 1489), a glittering late gothic miniature house, a combination of small-scale architecture, sculpture and painting, served for the preservation of relics. The long sides and the roof-ridge are richly ornamented with open-carved meshwork. The pointed gables of the short sides are crowned with a finial flanked by pinnacles. The four corner supports are adorned with statuettes. On one of the short sides two hospital sisters kneel beside the Virgin in a gothic choir. They have been identified as Jossine van Dudzele and Anna van der Moortele. Jossine van Dudzele became mother superior in 1489. On the other short side stands St. Ursula in a similar architectural decor. In her hand she holds the arrow with which she was martyred. Beneath her mantle shelters a group of virgins. On the long sides the pilgrimage of Ursula and the 11.000 Virgins to Rome is portrayed as though in a picture-story. The story is based on the 13th century 'Legenda aurea' by Jacob van Voragine. Ursula, a Breton princess, was asked in marriage by the King of England for his son. She accepted this proposal on con-

dition that she could make a pilgrimage to Rome. She was to convert ten virgins to this plan. Together they were each to bring a thousand virgins to the true faith, so that the company grew into the legendary 11.000 Virgins. In the first panel the company disembarks and passes through a gate into the city of Cologne in the background.

Various still-existing monuments are outlined against the sky. From left to right one can see the Bayen Tower, the Church of St. Severinus, the St. Martin's Tower and the choir of the uncompleted Dom. The continuation of the story is enacted in the house to the right where the saint spends the night. Through the open windows one can see the angel who predicts her martyrdom. In the second scene the journey continues to Basle. Everybody disembarks there and follows a winding path towards the Alps. To the left in the third scene one can see the way which the procession has taken in order to reach Rome. In the foreground a group of the pilgrims has reached its destination. Pope Cyriac blesses St. Ursula, who kneels reverently on the

The St. Ursula Shrine.
Detail from the sloping roof with an angel playing a lute.

The St. Ursula Shrine.
Detail from the sloping roof with an angel playing a portable organ.

Pages 74 - 79.
Long sides of the St. Ursula Shrine.

steps of a stone staircase. Through an arch one sees the sacraments being given to the pilgrims. On the other long side the return journey and the martyrdom are depicted. On its way back the company is attended by the pope and his retinue. In the left panel they board the ships which are moored outside the city gates of Basle. The two last scenes are enacted in front of the city of Cologne, of which a magnificent panoramic view is painted. The travellers are attacked by the Huns, who had captured the city at that time. Armed with arrows, spears and swords, the soldiers on the banks harass the retinue. After disembarking Ursula is led before the chief. Warriors parading in front of tents watch as one of them stretches his bow to shoot the saint. This executioner is probably Dschem, the brother of Sultan Bajazet II, as he was portrayed by Mantegna at his capture by the Christians in 1482. In the medaillons on the sloping roofs one sees in the centre once more the group of virgins and along the other sides an enthroned Virgin Mary. In each of the four tondos set into the painted tracery an angel is playing a musical instrument.

Numerous craftsmen contributed to the making of this magnificent gilded wooden house : sawyers, carpenters, carvers and upholsterers.

There has never been any doubt that the colourful miniaturesque panels are by Memling's hand. The pictures on the sloping roofs are atelier work. The shrine was intended to replace another reliquary (c. 1400). From the act of conveyance drawn up when the relics were transferred it can be deduced that the St. Ursula shrine was placed in the hospital church in 1489. It remained there until 1839 and only then left the old sick-ward so as to be housed in the Memling Museum. Until 1869 it continued to fulfill its original rôle and annually during the month of October it was still carried in procession to the church during the octave of St. Ursula. Because of the danger of damage the management of the Civic Almshouses asked that the shrine should henceforth not be moved. The relics were taken out of it and Memling's masterpiece became one of the museum's showpieces.

The Portrait of a Woman of 1480 is also named *The Sibylla Sambetha* on account of the inscriptions which appear on the painting. The text on the banderole refers to the prophecy of Christ's coming by the Persian Sibyl or Sibylla Sambetha. Both texts, on the banderole and in the renaissance cartouche, are however a 16th century addition. The sibyl or heathen prophetess was portrayed in quite a different manner in gothic art, with clothing of exotic appearance. Here however we see a young woman clothed in the fashion of the time. The black robe with a high girdle, the V-shaped cut out neck with a broad white collar filled with a red band, the partly plucked hair combed back and mounted in a cone, the draped and starched transparent veil, all point to the costume of the third quarter of the 15th century. It is an ideallized portrait whose rarified features nevertheless preserve the character of the person portrayed. In spite of the impression of absence and of gazing within herself, the illusion is created that this young woman is looking as though through an open window and in this manner seeking contact with the outside world. Nothing enables the portrait to be identified. The pendant with the little golden cross and the numerous rings on her fingers suggest that she is a member of the higher bourgeoisie. The panel was presented to the St. Julian's Hospital in the course of the 17th century, and after the closure of that institution in 1815 it was placed in the St. John's Hospital.

Portrait of a Woman or the Sibylla Sambetha, 1480.
Oak, oil, 38 × 26.5
The following inscription appears on the frame : 'ecce bestia conculcaberis, gignetur, dns in orbem terrarum et gremiv virginis erit salus gentium, invisibile verbv palpabitvr'.
The inscription in the cartouche reads as follows : 'Sibylla Sambetha Quae / e(s)t Persica, an : ante / Christ : nat : Z040'.
Inv. O.SJ174.I

SIBYLLA SAMBETHA QVÆ
ET PERSICA, AN: ANTE
CHRIST: NAT: 2040.

BESTIA CONCVLCABERIS, GIGNETVR, DNS IN ORBEM TERRARVM.
VIRGINIS ERIT SALVS GENTIVM, INVISIBILE VERBV PALPABITVR.

Diptych with the Virgin and Martin van Nieuwenhove, 1487.
Detail of the right-hand panel with the donor's patron saint. St. Martin is giving a piece of his cloak to a cripple.

Detail of the left-hand panel. The coat-of-arms and device of Martin van Nieuwenhove : 'il y a cause'. Both figures can be seen reflected in the mirror.

Detail of the left-hand panel. Through the window one sees a road winding through the landscape. This again helps to create the illusion of depth.

Diptych with the Virgin and Martin van Nieuwenhove, 1487.
Oak, oil, 44 × 33 (per panel).
The following inscription appears on the frame : 'hoc . opus . fieri . fecit . Martinus . De Newenhoven . Anno . dm . 148 . ano . vero . etatis . sue . 23'.
Inv. O.SJ178.1

The diptych with the Virgin and Martin van Nieuwenhove (1487) is inspired by the devotional panels with half-figures which are also to be found in the work of Rogier Van der Weyden. The Virgin with the apple in her hand and the infant Christ on a brocade cushion is one of Memling's best known madonna types. The jewels of the discreet diadem, the precious stones on the V-neck and the fur of the sleeves are all delicately applied expressions of luxury which testify to the importance of the figure but do not disturb its serenity. The coats-of-arms and inscriptions enable us to identify the donor as the 23-year old Martin van Nieuwenhove, a member of a prominent Brugean family. In full consciousness of his human dignity, he is portrayed in equal size next to the Virgin. He is in fact in the same room, as is evidenced by the convex mirror with the reflections of both bodies. By depicting the walls of the interior on both panels in a different perspective the corner of a room is suggested, which gives the spectator the illusion of being one of the company. The landscape which is evoked through the open windows is designed to give depth to both panels.

In 1640 this diptych was still in the possession of the Van Nieuwenhove family. A few years later it was presented to the St. Julian's Hospice. In 1815, together with the 'Portrait of a Woman', it was added to the St. John's Hospital collection.

The other paintings

A HIGHLY VARIED COLLECTION, BROUGHT together between the 15th and the 19th century, is preserved here. The nature of the collection does not make it possible to offer an evenly built up survey of painting in general or even of local painting. Although the earliest works are mostly by anonymous masters, they can in every case, due to iconography or style, be considered as Brugean work.

For the later periods, from the 17th century onwards, there are also paintings to be seen here by the most important artists who worked in Bruges. It is noticeable that certain genres are better represented than others. Most of the paintings have religious subjects. They were purchased in order to decorate the church, to be placed on altars or as devotional panels in order to stimulate religious feelings. There are numerous individual portraits, mostly of personalities who had a connection with this institution. Also important are the iconographic pictures which evoke the history of the hospital and sometimes provide data concerning buildings and furnishings with photographic exactness.

Anonymous, Antwerp (?), 2nd half 16th century.
Marriage of Cana (detail).
Panel, oil, 102 × 162
Inv. O.SJ163.I

Anonymous, Flanders, 17th century.
Portrait of Francisco Pardo, guardian of St. Julian's Hospital,
1606 - 1615, 1604.
Panel, oil, 51 × 39
Inv. O.SJ123.I

Anonymous, Flanders, beginning 17th century.
Portret of Joris van Brakele, guardian of St. Julian's Hospital,
1568 - 1606.
Panel, oil, 53 × 41
Inv. O.SJ120.I

The Portraits of the Guardians

THE PORTRAITS OF THE GUARDIANS MAY be considered as one series. A first series was made for the hospital and has always been kept here. From the second half of the 13th century two representatives per institution were appointed by the city magistrate and charged with supervision on the spot. In the 17th and 18th centuries in particular an aristocracy of officials had formed itself in Bruges, which had the monopoly of city government in its hands. Thus one often finds among those portrayed here members of the same family and people who must have known one another well. After the French Revolution it was only the presidents of the administration set up at the time who got a portrait in the gallery. This tradition is still observed.

The oldest portrait, of 'Johannes Despars', painted by an anonymous master, dates from 1618. With few exceptions all the later portraits of guardians have been preserved. They are mostly the work of Brugean painters. Some of these artists had also achieved renown far beyond the limits of the city. They are all conceived in accordance with the same principle. They are all bust portraits and the earliest ones are framed in a medallion. Under the painting itself an inscription has in each case been added. The series gives a good idea of the evolution of the portrait in the course of time, with its high and low points. This collection is a valuable aid in the study of local social and political history, in the study of fashion and in the knowledge of genealogy and heraldry.

A second series originates from St. Julian's. This was begun in the course of the 16th century and ends with the French Revolution, at which time the hospital was closed. This series is not as complete as the former, for about one third of the portraits are missing. Various paintings seem to have been adapted later so that one gets the impression that originally they were created separately and later turned into a series by framing them in the same manner. Although no explanatory texts appear underneath, various personages can be identified with the help of titles and coats-of-arms. Especially among the older ones can be found some outstanding examples of portrait painting.

Anonymous, Flanders, end 17th century.
Portrait of Karel de Meulenaere, guardian of St. Julian's Hospital, between 1699 and 1705, 1699.
Canvas, oil, 50.5 × 38.5
Inv. O.SJ131.I

Anonymous, Flanders, 18th century.
Portrait of Pieter Antoon de Peneranda, guardian of St. Julian's Hospital, 1769.
Canvas, oil, 47 × 36.5
Inv. O.SJ134.I

N. Lytton (1876 - 1951).
Portrait of Baron Ernest van Caloen, hospital guardian, 1931.
Canvas, oil, 62.5 × 51
Inv. O.SJ100.I

J. Van Oost the Elder (1603 - 1671), attributed.
Portrait of hospital guardian Hermanus van Volden, 1633.
Panel, oil, 63.5 × 49.5
Inv. O.SJ83.I

Devotional panels and other paintings

THE *TWO PANELS WITH THE ANNUNCIATION* (end 15th century) by an anonymous master were originally the lateral panels of a triptych. The conception draws on the 15th century grisaille paintings which were always used for the decoration of the outer panels. The figures can be considered as an imitation of sculpture. They are not however placed in niches, but in an interior. Imitation marble can be seen on the frame.

Two anonymous devotional paintings in which the Holy Trinity is represented are very interesting on account of the iconography. The first type shows a *Mercy-seat with John the Baptist and to the right John the Evangelist* (end 15th century). This theme with God the Father enthroned and holding the crucified Christ in his hands goes back to the 12th century. Normally the Holy Spirit in the form of a dove appears between the two figures. During the late middle ages the cult of the Holy Trinity was very popular. The clumsy wooden figures of the saints, however, suggest folk art. This colourful scene nevertheless has great charm. The landscape, although painted in very rudimentary fashion, points to the end of the 15th century. The panel adorned the chapel of the 'Rooms Couvent', one of Bruges' oldest almshouses (14th century). In about 1929 it was transferred to the museum of the Civic Almshouses.

In the *Triptych with a representation of the Trinity* one sees a second type of Trinitarian Piëtà, in which God the Father on His throne bears the dead Christ on his knees. Here the dove sits on the Father's shoulder. The iconography is inspired by a prototype ascribed to the master of Flémalle, alias Campin. It was very popular at the courts of the Burgundian dukes among others. St. John and the Virgin are here portrayed as mediators. Their presence has its origin in mystical and devotional literature. On the lateral panels the same saints are depicted as on Memling's 'Adrian Reins Triptych', namely Adrian, Barbara, Mary of Egypt and Wilgeforte. But the middle panel here shows the 'Compassion' of the Father, where with Memling the counterpart is to be seen, namely 'Compassion of the Mother or the Pieta'. The costume allows us to date this painting approximately to the first quarter of the 16th century. Pithy details of form and colour in the clothing, together with the hazy handling of faces, suggest the circle of Adriaan Isenbrant (b. ca. 1490 - d. 1551). Taking the iconography into account, this triptych was most probably made for the hospital.

Anonymous, Flanders, end 15th century.
Two panels with the Annunciation.
Panel, oil, 76.9 × 28
Inv. O.SJ185.I

Anonymous, Bruges, beginning 16th century.
Triptych with a representation of the Trinity.
Panel, oil, 60 × 43 (centre), 60 × 21 (lateral panels).
Inv. O.SJ187.I

Anonymous, Flanders, end 15th century.
Mercy seat with left John the Baptist and right John the Evangelist.
Panel, oil, 118.5 × 55
Inv. O.SJ196.I

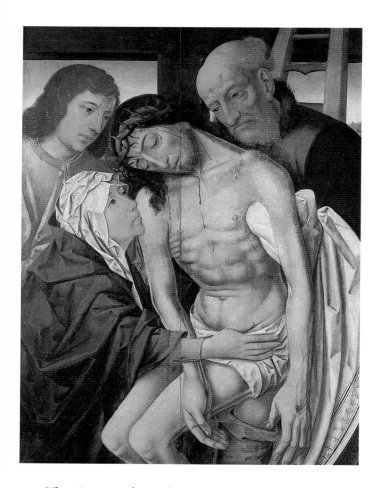

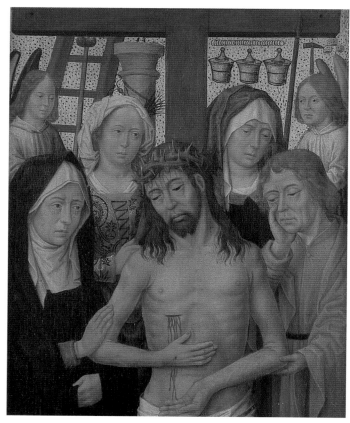

The *Descent from the Cross* (15th century) after a
lost original by Rogier Van der Weyden must have had
a great success in Bruges, since various other replicas
have been preserved. The vertical Christ figure in the
middle of the composition and the close-up technique
which has been used must have struck the passer-by.
Such devotional panels claimed attention for the suffering and death of Christ. Somewhat later is another
Descent from the Cross which may have enjoyed even
greater approval and which goes back to a panel by
Hugo Van der Goes. From the details of the clothing
the painting can be dated to the beginning of the 16th
century.

Closely associated in theme is the picture of *The
Man of Sorrows surrounded by the instruments of the
passion.* It too is an 'Imago Piëtatis' based on medieval
mystical literature. The spectator is directly confronted
with the figures who lament Christ's suffering and
death, one of the essential motifs of medieval devotion.

The two anonymous *Panels with scenes from the
Finding of the Cross* also originally belonged to a triptych or to a retable. On the outer side the story of the
finding of the cross by St. Helen is colourfully illustrated. On the inner sides can be seen a very interesting
portrayal of Job, surrounded by musicians. The original frame is still preserved. Until the middle of the last
century these paintings were kept in the Bogarden
school where the orphans lived.

After Rogier Van der Weyden, 15th century.
The Descent from the Cross.
Panel, oil, 84.8 × 64
Inv. O.SJ186.I

Anonymous, beginning 16th century.
The Man of Sorrows surrounded by instruments of the Passion.
Panel, oil, 39.1 × 31.5
Inv. O.SJ184.I

After Hugo Van der Goes, beginning 16th century.
The Descent from the Cross.
Panel, oil, 65.5 × 82.3
Inv. O.SJ190.I

Anonymous, beginning 16th century.
Panels with scenes from the Finding of the Cross.
Panel, oil, 93.9 × 42.3 and 94.5 × 41.2
Inv. O.SJ183(a) and (b).1

The *Diptych with the Carrying of the Cross on the left and the portrait of a friar on the right* (1522) is ascribed to Jan Provoost (b. 1465 - d. 1529). Although this well-known master is considered to have been an interesting innovator in Brugean painting, this diptych with half figures is conceived somewhat traditionally, especially as regards the theme. The *Carrying of the Cross* is inspired by the Ghent 'Carrying of the Cross' by Hieronymus Bosch (b. ca. 1450 - d. 1516). The close-up technique here helps to accentuate the drama of suffering very sharply. Interesting is the scene on the reverse side with the skull in the niche. A 'memento mori' or 'consider, O man'. The following rebus appears on the original frame : 'Dur est la pensée de la / / mort / / bonnet de penser a mi (moi)'. An entreaty on the part of the donor to continue to remember him. An entreaty which also encourages one to meditate on the 'vanitas' or transitoriness of earthly life.

During the meal of *Jesus in the house of Simon* the elegant Mary Magdalen comes to sprinkle Christ's feet with tears and dry them with her hair. This iconography is based on a text which appears in the four gospels. The composition is a free recapitulation of the original ascribed to Dirk Bouts (Gemäldegalerie der Staatliche Museen in Berlin). The interior with its renaissance-style attributes enables it to be dated in the first half of the 16th century.

The *Good Samaritan* is an exciting work by an anonymous master. Various scenes from the parable are portrayed in a refined and whimsical landscape. Our attention is drawn to the samaritan who is looking after the victim in the foreground. The involved composition is very harmoniously balanced. The figures in the foreground are plastic in concept and well drawn. The distorted expression of the wounded man creates a dramatic impression. The colours are cool and everything is painted with a smooth technique. The style enables the panel to be dated in the middle of the 16th century and ascribed to a follower of van Scorel (b. 1495 - d. 1562).

The *Marriage of Cana* (2nd half 16th century) relates how Christ changed water into wine. This episode too is based on a gospel text. It was a very popular subject during the middle ages. The painting, by an unknown master, bears resemblances to works from Antwerp. It originates from St. Elizabeth's girls' school.

Page 92.
Circle of Dirk Bouts, first half 16th century.
Jesus in the house of Simon.
Panel, oil, 70.5 × 52
Inv. O.SJ188.I

Anonymous, circle of J. Van Scorel, 2nd half 16th century.
The Good Samaritan.
Panel, oil, 100.3 × 70.7
Inv. O.SJ192.I

Jan Provoost (1465 - 1529).
Diptych with left the Carrying of the Cross and right the Portrait of a Friar, 1522.
Reverse side with the rebus.

Diptych with left the Carrying of the Cross and right the Portrait of a Friar, 1522.
Panel, oil, 49.8 × 40 (per panel).
The following text appears on the frame : 'Francisci (Cordula) traxit ad se plurima (corda) Anno Domini XV XXIJ. Fueram annorum LIIIJ'.
Inv. O.SJ191.I

Jacob Van Oost the Elder (1603 - 1671).
The Ascension into Heaven of St. Apollonia, ca. 1660.
Canvas, oil, 262 × 169
Inv. O.SJ252.I

Claeissens atelier (?), 2nd half 16th century.
Rest on the Flight to Egypt.
Panel, oil, 62 × 49.4
Inv. O.SJ181.I

Page 95.
Pieter Claeissens The Younger (? - 1623).
The Carrying of the Cross, 1616.
Panel, oil, 108.5 × 137.3
Inv. O.SJ162.I

Page 96.
Statue of Cornelius.
Detail of the head (14th century).

Page 97.
Virgin Mary porch (end of the 13th century).

The *Rest on the Flight to Egypt* was to provide the occasion for portrayals of a madonna in a landscape which were very popular in Bruges and are inspired by a prototype by Gerard David (b. ca. 1460 - d. 1523). Although some discoloration appears, both the colours and the style suggest the work of the Claeissens family who were very active in Bruges from the second half of the 16th century. The *Carrying of the Cross* of 1616 is certainly by Pieter Claeissens the Younger (b. ? - d. 1623). The procession which left Jerusalem for Golgotha was a very popular subject in the late middle ages and was represented enthusiastically in the Southern Netherlands during the 16th century. It inspired highly narrative interpretations. Here one sees less incidental scenes, so that one's attention is drawn rather to the falling Christ. The ochre colours of the landscape are typical for this painter. Several canvasses are ascribed on stylistic grounds to Jacob van Oost the Elder (b. 1603 -

d. 1671). This master stamped his seal on the Brugean painting school of the 17th century. His name appears regularly in the accounts, but sometimes it is only possible to guess which commission he was in fact being paid for. Apart from producing important paintings he also created some less remarkable work. Among other things he polychromed the herb-boxes of the pharmacy. One of his most important monumental paintings is *The Madonna surrounded by Saints*. It was placed on the high altar in 1637 to replace Hans Memling's masterpiece, which had to make way for the new baroque decoration. The subjects are to some extent related. Here too a 'Sacra Conversazione' is depicted with the madonna in the centre. There is also a secondary theme, where the Virgin places the mitre on Augustine's head. Augustine is the patron saint of the convent community.

Here too the standing patron saints of the hospital flank the Virgin. The four other saints are the tradi-tional patrons of the plague : Sebastian with the arrow, Roche with the wound, Abbot Antony with the staff and Adrian as a warrior. In previous years the plague had caused ravages in the city and here too it was to claim many victims before the disease was brought under control at the end of the same century. The composition is well balanced. The enthroned Virgin is placed somewhat out of the axis, which allows the saints to be put in well-poised groups opposite one another. The use of colossal order for the architectural decor, the play of light and the colours belong to the baroque repertoire.

Bands of angels accompany the *Ascension into Heaven of St. Apollonia* (ca. 1657). The form of the painting suggests that it was intended for an altar retable. In 1657 an altar was dedicated to this popular saint in a chapel erected in the Mariastraat next to the sculptured entrance porch. This oratory was demolished in the middle of the last century.

Sculpture

THE O.C.M.W COLLECTION COMPRISES numerous sculptures made of the most varied materials : different types of stone, plain and polychromed wood and ivory. Most of them date from the gothic period (13th - beginning 16th century). Some of these sculptures were certainly commissioned by St. John's. The study of medieval Brugean sculpture in general, however, leaves many questions unanswered. Yet some very interesting works of art are preserved here, which can be ascribed to Bruges and serve as reference for further research.

Of exceptional interest is the *Virgin Mary Porch* built at the end of the 13th century against the existing street-facade of the middle sick-ward (beginning 13th century). It is one of the few ensembles to be seen in Bruges and in the whole of Flanders. Its present-day appearance with the imposing limestone canopy is a result of the restoration of 1911-13 after a design by architect Coomans (b. 1871 - d. 1937). The original sculpture which is grouped under the pointed arches was not only restored, but the entire tympanum was completed by sculptor Remi Rooms.

'The death of the Virgin Mary' is represented twice, on the left in the company of angels and on the right with Christ in the midst of the apostles and above that 'the Deësis group' and 'the Coronation of the Virgin'. Small figures of the apostles stand in the archivolts. The iconography is a combination of the two most common types of porch in Northern France : the Virgin Mary porch and the Last Judgement porch. The Deësis group with the Christ of the Last Judgement flanked by St. John and the Virgin belongs to the second type. The style is also influenced by French examples of the high-gothic period. Expressions of this are the striving for a realistic rendering, obtained by the exercise of three-dimensionality, and the occurence of a plastically broken and contrasting play of folds. Nevertheless these French examples were interpreted. The figures give a more miniature effect and the forms are more schematic. This points to the work of a local Brugean (or even Tournai) atelier, active at the end of the 13th century.

The *Standing Madonna with the Christ Child writing* in polychromed wood is one of the very rare remaining pieces which, on account of the iconography and the style, can be ascribed to a Brugean sculptor of the period (ca. 1375-1390). The theme of the 'Christ Child writing' was very popular in Flanders and is linked to the work of redemption. This iconography was certainly not unfamiliar in Bruges and other examples of it were to be seen in the Church of St. Donatian and on the facade of the Town Hall. The Madonna is considered as a local example of the so-called 'soft style'. The elegant bodily forms and the finely cut, gentle face point to this style. In contrast the sober drapery with a very clearly arranged schema is a very characteristic regional attribute.

The origin of the monumental *Cornelius statue* poses less problems. The imposing and majestic figure of the pope is almost completely gilded and polychromed. Cornelius can be recognized by the tiara and cross-staff and by the horn which refers to his name. Together with other saints he played an important part in hospital life as a 'healer'. This sculpture is regarded as a basic work for the knowledge of medieval Brugean sculpture. The monumental, broadly chiselled, outstretched body and the severe front-facing seated posture are also to be found in other examples. This severity is softened by the mobility of the drapery and especially by the delicate polychrome of the features. These last stylistic attributes can be situated in the 'soft style' which had great success all over Europe around 1400. In 1394 the Cornelius guild signed a contract with the hospital authorities for the use of the chapel adjoining the church. At that time important works were being carried out to rearrange the interior, so that it is not surprising that the statue was ordered at that moment. The stylistic attributes do not contradict this hypothesis.

Standing Madonna with the Christ Child writing.
Attributed to a Brugean atelier, about 1375-1390.
Wood and polychrome, h 63.
Inv. O.SJ224.V

Statue of Cornelius. *Bruges, end 14th century.*
Oak, gilt and polychrome, h 166.5.
Inv. O.SJ157.V

Seated Madonna.
France or Flanders, about 1350.
Ivory, traces of polychrome and gilt, h 20.
Inv. O.SJ222.VIII

Polyptych of the Virgin.
Flanders, about 1450-1500 and 19th century.
Ivory, gilt and painted, 27.5 × 14.3 × 4.1 (centre),
27.7 × 11.5 (lateral panels).
Inv. O.SJ.221.VIII

The *Small Reliquary Shrine of St. Ursula* is the humble predecessor of Memling's splendid masterpiece. It is a very small, rectangular miniature house finished with a saddle-roof and small crenelles. It is a combination of painting and sculpture. 'Ursula with the 11,000 Virgins' under her mantle is chiselled out in relief. Together with other saints St. John the Baptist appears again here on the long side. On the short sides stands his attribute 'The Lamb of God'. Here too, therefore, the link with the hospital is clear. It is dated about 1380-1400 and is one of the only remaining painted panels in Bruges from that period. The naïve, refined miniaturesque personages are examples of a more artless interpretation of the 'soft style'.

A *Sitting Madonna* in ivory is dated the middle of the 14th century. This gem was originally polychromed and still bears traces of gilt. Paris was an important centre for ivory work at this period. It has not, however, been proved that the little statue was imported. Ivory carvers were also active in our region. There are insufficient clear stylistic data for the piece to be localized exactly.

The *Polyptych* in polychromed and gilded ivory has given rise to various hypotheses regarding its date. In the middle an 'Enthroned Madonna' is to be seen. On the lateral panels are carved scenes from the life of the Virgin. Graceful angels playing music accompany these scenes. The lateral panels and the central panel differ greatly in style. The architectural forms and the treatment of the figures on the lateral panels suggest a 15th century origin. The 'Enthroned Madonna' on the other hand resembles more closely examples from the first half of the 14th century. Differences however can be observed, so that the hypothesis has been put forward that it could here be a question of a 19th century copy.

'Wall tabernacles' are fairly rare in Flanders. They were either the victims of iconoclasm or were demolished during the Counter-Reformation, when tabernacles found a place on the altar itself. In the St. John's Hospital there are still two to be seen, which is quite exceptional. The *Wall tabernacle* (ca. 1410-1420) from the Cornelius chapel with its blind-niche tracery and its buttresses is a fine example of late-gothic miniature architecture. Under a pointed arch is to be seen a representation of the 'Garden of Olives', a fine example of miniature sculpture, as are also the angel musicians which serve as consoles for the buttresses. The small niches of these buttresses also contained sculpture, similar to that which can be seen on Memling's St. Ursula shrine. Unfortunately the sculptures here have disappeared.

The Wall tabernacle or the Tower of the Sacraments of the church is much more monumental. It is composed of various horizontal indentations adorned with blind-niches, open-work and floral motifs in flamboyant gothic. Here too there was once small sculptural work in the niches and on the buttresses. Only the 'Garden of Olives' and a statuette of St. John remain.

The magnificently wrought small copper doors were paid for in 1477, so that we can say with certainty that the wall tabernacle forms part of the church interior which was created in the late gothic period.

The collection also boasts a number of statuettes in alabaster. A *Visitation* and an *Apostle figure* are ascribed to the same atelier. The theme of the meeting of the Virgin and Elizabeth is portrayed in a touching way. The numerous elegant folds of the drapery are very graceful and typical for a series of statuettes which are grouped round the so-called 'Master of the Retable of Rimini'. A small apostle figure can be compared with this. The hypothesis has been put forward that this atelier in Northern France or Flanders was active in about 1430. The making of alabaster statuettes is generally considered to be an English activity. There must certainly have been a prolific production in England between the 14th and the 16th centuries. But there are traces which suggest that alabaster was also worked in our regions. Unfortunately there is too little known data for us to come to any definite conclusions about this. Thus it is assumed that the *Peter and Paul with the Veronica cloth* (ca. 1430-50) and the *Risen Christ* (ca. 1430-50) could have been made in this country.

Wall tabernacle.
Bruges, 1410 - 1420.
Sandstone, 180 × 80
Inv. O.SJ751.VI

Wall tabernacle.
Bruges, 1477.
Sandstone, polychromed.
Inv. O.SJ746.VI

Visitation.
Northern France or Flanders, atelier of the Master of the retable of Rimini, 1430 - 1440.
Alabaster, h 38.
Inv. O.SJ296.VI

Peter and Paul.
Flanders, 1430 - 1450.
Alabaster, traces of polychrome, h 19.2.
Inv. O.SJ220.VI

Apostle.
Northern France or South Netherlands, atelier of the Master of the retable of Rimini, 1430 - 1440.
Alabaster, h 23.7.
Inv. O.SJ219.VI

Risen Christ.
Flanders, 1430 - 1450.
Alabaster, polychrome, h 19.5.
Inv. O.SJ217.VI

A whole series of 15th century wooden statues has been preserved. A *St. Antony* of about 1410-20 can still be seen in a niche of the church.

A splendid example of the 'soft style' which distinguishes a number of refined and extremely charming works of art dated about 1400 is the *Standing Madonna* in fruit-wood. The combination of the jaunty posture with the rolling of the hips, the inward monumentality and the abstract play of lines of the mantle points to a mature stage of this style and allows the work to be dated around 1410-20.

The *Pietà* (ca. 1430-50) shows in the general drapery and modelling of the Christ figure some kinship with the 'soft style'. This statue, however, with the angular form of its folds, is an interesting example of a development in style which in Bruges too was to lead to the 'hard style' of the late gothic.

The colourful *Christmas cradle* (1425-50) is a miniature piece of furniture which illustrates the devotion of late-medieval man. Few examples have been preserved. A moveable cradle is hung under a little canopy. The cradle was rocked during the Christmas service.

Few medieval 'Calvary groups' are to be found in Bruges. The origin of the *Calvary group* to be found here on the premises is taken on stylistic grounds to go back to 1450-75. The hypothesis has been put forward that this group was ordered as a triumphal cross for the church. It is possible to defend this supposition since the church was rebuilt and rearranged from 1472.

The posture of the *Two gliding Angels* (ca. 1450-1500) suggests that they originally belonged to one ensemble. The hands are probably gripping the frame of a Marianum. Such a Marianum is still preserved in the St. Leonard's Church in Zoutleeuw. It is unlikely that both these originally polychromed angel figures originated in Brabant.

Angel.
Flanders, between 1450 - 1500.
Oak, polychrome and gilt, h 87. Inv. O.SJ223.V

From the left to the right.
Standing Madonna.
Flanders, 1410 - 1420.
Fruitwood, h 46.5. Inv. O.SJ215.V

Pieta.
Flanders, 1430 - 1450.
Oak, polychrome, h 67. Inv. O.SJ216.V

St. Barbara.
Flanders, ca. 1500, h 69. Inv. O.SJ218.V

Christmas cradle.
Flanders, 1425 - 1450.
Wood, polychrome and gilt, h 60.
The embroidery and the silver Christ child date from 1714. Inv. O.SJ81.V

Madonna under canopy.
Brussels, 1500 - 1510.
Wood, polychrome and gilt, h 27. Inv. O.SJ225.V

St. Hieronymus.
Flanders, 1513 - 1514.
Oak, over-painting, h 97.5.
Inv. O.SJ732.V

St. Antony.
Flanders, 1410 - 1420.
Oak, paintwork, h 92.
Inv. O.SJ731.V

St. John the Evangelist.
Flanders, 1513 - 1514.
Oak, over-painting, h 95.
Inv. O.SJ730.V

St. Augustine.
Flanders, 18th century.
Wood, over-painting, h 161.
Inv. O.SJ734.V

Page 106.
Buffet cupboard.
Bruges, 1678. Detail with the representation of St. John the Baptist.
Inv. O.SJ80.VII

Madonna.
Beginning 18th century.
Wood, polychrome, h 110.
Inv. O.SJ387.V

A *St. Barbara* (late 15th - early 16th century) in a graceful mobile posture, leaning against her attribute, the tower, has a type of face which betrays the work of a Flemish atelier. A fine example of precious miniature sculpture is the gilded *Madonna under Canopy.* The richly made open-work architecture points to Brabant as being the origin. In the accounts for 1513-14 payment is mentioned for carving and upholstering two statues : a *St. John the Evangelist* and the patriarch *Hieronymus.* Both statues have been preserved in the church. They both have voluminous drapery with plastically created broken folds. The features are realistically carved. It is not possible, however, to attribute both statues to the same sculptor. They were later painted white.

In the church can be seen two statues of saints of a later date, which have a special link with the hospital. *St. Apollonia* with pincers and martyr's palm in her hands is made of whitepainted and gilded gold. The silver pincers and palm were presented by sister Rosalia Berlamont, sextoness, in 1861. The statue must have been carved in the 17th century. A *St. Augustine*, patron saint of the Augustine sisters, stands on a similar socle to *St. Apollonia.* The figure is tall and lengthy. The somewhat cramped posture and the barely agitated, finely creased handling of the folds of his bishop's clothing cause one to suspect that this sculpture was ordered in the 18th century.

In contrast with the previous sculpture the *Madonna* of the beginning of the 18th century is an outstanding example of mobility. The S-shaped bent body, the floundering Christ child and the numerous and complicated playful folds give anything but a static effect. It is still completely polychromed. The origin of this statue is not known either.

Furniture

A GREAT VARIETY OF FURNITURE, ESPECIALLY of the 16th and 17th centuries, has been preserved here. Storage and seating furniture, intended for the living quarters, the household, the sick-wards, the pharmacy, or coming from other institutions. Although these show some traces of wear and tear as a result of constant use, it may generally be claimed that a number of authentic pieces of furniture have been handed down to us in fairly good condition. The purchase of these items is to be found repeatedly in the accounts, but it is difficult to determine precisely which objects are referred to, since the descriptions are too summary and the name does not always make it clear which type exactly is concerned.

Some of them can be labelled as typical Brugean work and these serve as a reference point in the study of local furniture production. Most of them are made of oak, with the exception of some examples imported from abroad. The church furniture is equally interesting. The choir-benches, of 1661, have definite Brugean characteristics, with the plastically conceived sculpture of the figures and of the motifs carved in the genuine shining oak. Several of these ornaments are also to be found in the bourgeois furniture of this period.

The beds and alcoves have unfortunately disappeared. They were replaced regularly. In the archives one finds that new beds were acquired during virtually every period. Thanks to these sources and also to the iconographic documents a fairly good idea can be obtained of the appearance of these pieces of furniture, which constituted the most important contents of the sick-wards.

Little furniture of the 15th century has been preserved. One of the oldest items is a very precious article imported from Northern Italy : a *small chest* in cedarwood. On the front there are figures, animals and tendrils carved in a linear manner with great feeling for elegance. Traces of red and green filling-paste show that items of furniture of this kind were polychromed. The scenes are inspired by the courtly literature of the period.

An interesting example of a 're-used' piece of furniture is the 15th century cupboard which was later converted into a *charity-table*. The original structure of the furniture, which originally had an open under-frame, can still be clearly recognized. Charity-tables used to be mounted at the back of the churches. At regular intervals the table was 'dressed'. In this way those in need could obtain provisions or clothing in exchange for lead charity-pennies. Similar items of furniture came into the collection after the French Revolution, when the working of the parochial charities was taken over by the 'Charity Office'. Two *double-door cupboards* of the end of the 15th century or beginning of the 16th century can be considered as typical gothic Flemish pieces

Alms table.
Flanders, small 15th century cupboard, later adapted.
Oak, 95.5 × 122 × 69.8
Inv. O.SJ6.VII

Two-door cupboards
Flanders, ca. 1500.
Oak, 109.5 × 148.5 × 59.2. Inv. O.SJ7.VII
Oak, 105 × 151 × 68.5. Inv. O.SJ10.VII

of storage furniture. The two doors and the sides of the first item are decorated with scrolled panels. The iron-work is authentic. The original leaf has unfortunately disappeared. A second example is still in perfect condition. The doors exhibit a variation on the X-motif. The leaf with moulding is in this case preserved.

The *two-storey cupboards* (16th century) are already items of renaissance furniture. Above they each have several bays and below they have two doors. With one of these pieces one still finds the gothic scrolled panels on the sides. The decoration of the doors with highly stylized motifs has evolved further. Here too the iron-work is still original. A second example is also, as regards the ornamentation, a good example of a Flemish renaissance piece of furniture. As a result of stylization the older designs have evolved into circles suggestive of renaissance medallions. The diamond shape at the top with the inscribed figure in high relief is typical of the new style, as is also the door-needle underneath.

The 17th century production is amply represented. Various types of *store-cupboards* are to be seen in the

Two-storey cupboard. *Flanders, 16th century.*
Oak, 105 × 185 × 53. Inv. O.SJ16.VII

museum. These were used to store provisions and were thus functional items of furniture rather than show-cupboards, and were mostly decorated with simple mouldings. The open-worked panels are a characteristic feature. These are fashioned of diagonally woven bars, often with a copper nail-head on the intersections. There are also hanging-cupboards, low store-cupboards and pieces of furniture with various storeys. The standing examples have a hinged frame underneath which can be folded upwards for cleaning purposes.

Store-cupboard.
Flanders, 17th century.
Oak, 85 × 65 × 35. Inv. O.SJ17.VII

Two-storey cupboard.
Flanders, 16th century.
Oak, 173 × 146 × 68. Inv. O.SJ39.VII

Chest.
Flanders, 17th century.
Oak, 60 × 113 × 54. Inv. O.SJ524.VII

The *buffets* are typical pieces of show furniture. They all have a clearly divided upper and lower part. This is achieved by moulding and by richly sculptured drawers. The large cupboards have four doors, the smaller ones two. The lower doors are in each case overlaid with profiled geometric moulding round a central motif. In the upper doors there are often entire scenes chiselled in bas-relief. The fully plastic sculpture on the door-posts and drawers comes from a highly varied repertoire which is combined in different ways : socles and canopies harbouring little figures, twisted columns, angel heads, garlands of fruit and many other motifs. One of the most representative examples is the buffet cupboard of 1678. The hospital coat-of-arms makes it clear that the piece of furniture was made for this hospital. Elizabeth, Michael and Dorothy can be seen on the upper doorposts. Augustine, patron saint of the convent community, decorates the lower doors together with John the Baptist. The most picturesque scenes, however, are to be seen on the oblong upper doors where the pharmacy is portrayed on the left and the sick-ward on the right.

In the guardians' room a smaller model is to be found, and the link with the hospital is equally clear : St. Augustine and his mother St. Monica appear on the door-posts. The Brugean origin of all these buffet cupboards can scarcely be doubted.

Buffet cupboard.
Bruges, 17th century.
Oak, 133 × 164 × 64
Inv. O.SJ20.VII

Buffet cupboard. *Bruges, 1678.*
Detail with representation of the sick-ward.
Oak, 144.5 × 161.5 × 63.5. Inv. O.SJ80.VII

Small two-storey cupboard.
Bruges, 1693.
Oak, 113 × 83 × 53.5. Inv. O.SJ203.VII

Small two-storey cupboard.
Bruges, 17th century.
Oak, 122.5 × 87 × 67.5. Inv. O.SJ207.VII

From the remarkable collection of *chests* two examples have been selected here. These frame-built items of furniture, whose struts, members and posts are fastened together by dowelled joints, served to store the sisters' outfits and were made at the time of their entry. Inside they often have small trays under the hinged lid.

One sometimes finds little devotional prints pasted inside these pieces. Some of them are quite copiously decorated, such as the example with scale-motifs on the framework and with mouldings worked on the panels. Others are simpler and bear initials and a date. This is the case with a chest of 1717 with the initials M.P. : Marie Potvliet. This sister entered on 18th May 1717.

Besides the large 18th century refectory *tables* there are also smaller ones to be seen which mostly date from the 17th century. A good example is the table from the guardians' room with its four baluster-shaped legs and the planks underneath for greater strength. Under the table-top there are two sliding leaves.

Various baroque *chairs and armchairs*, known as 'Spanish leather chairs', were purchased for St. John's. Most of them have legs with vase-joints joined by pro-filed planks. The backs and seats are uphostered in leather. In some cases the gilt hospital coat-of-arms was printed on the back as a house-mark. It is remarkable that in spite of the intensive use of these chairs so many examples have survived.

Chest.
Flanders, 17th century.
Oak, 67 × 113.5 × 54
This chest belonged to Marie Potvliet.
Inv. O.SJ516.VII

Detail buffet cupboard with musician.
Bruges, 17th century.
Inv. O.SJ20.VII

Store-cupboard.
Flanders, 17th century.
Oak, 110 × 183 × 52.5
Inv. O.SJ35.VII

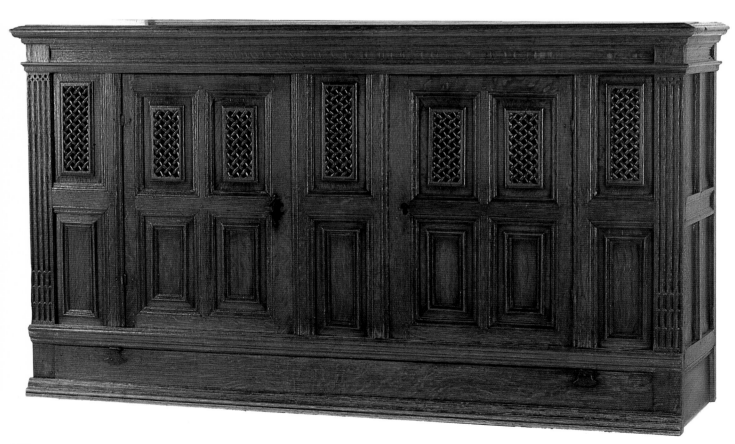

Relic ostensory.
Bruges, Jacques De Cantere jr., 1619 - 1620.
Silver, h 33.
This relic-holder with horizontal glass cylinder can be compared with the similar model made by the same master to preserve the remains of St. Apollonia. In this model the relics of various saints are to be found. Under the little canopy stands St. John the Baptist.
Inv. O.SJ817.X

Relic ostensory.
Bruges, Hendrik Van Ockerhout, ca. 1650 - 1660.
Silver, h 41.1.
Inv. O.SJ818.X

Relic ostensory.
Bruges, Jacques De Cantere jr., 1620.
Silver, h 35.5.
Relics of St. Apollonia. On the foot is engraved the name of sister Jaqueminken Gloribus (d. 1638) and 'Sint-Janshospitaal Brugge'.
Inv. O.SJ816.X

Relic ostensory.
Bruges, Jan Peperseele, 1630.
Silver, h 34.
Relics of various saints. On the small columns statuettes of St. Elizabeth of Hungary and a Madonna.
Inv. O.SJ815.X

Metal

IF ALL THE SILVER WHICH WAS PRESENTED to or bought by the St. John's Hospital in the course of time had been preserved, a magnificent treasure-chamber could be filled with it. As far back as the 15th century the church possessed an extensive wealth of silver consisting of chalices, ciboria and reliquaries. Here too the precious metal was demanded in difficult times. But a remarkable number of objects have still been preserved which can be attributed to Brugean masters. Chalices, monstrances, ampullae, censers, candlesticks, wall-arms, in short a highly varied collection of liturgical utensils which illustrates many centuries of the silversmith's art. About twenty items which originate from the Bogarden school in Brugge were also deposited here in 1883. The greatest part is kept in the convent and only the ostensories for relics are to be found in the large wall-tabernacle of the church. They testify to the lively devotion which existed here for certain saints and which was stimulated by brotherhoods.

The oldest is the *horn relic of St. Cornelius* (16th century). The horn shape refers to the saint's attribute, a so-called speaking attribute, derived from his name. The other examples have a horizontal or vertical glass cylinder in which the relics can be seen. This is contained in the precious metal and rests on a decorated stem and multi-lobed foot. On the cylinder a canopy is usually mounted, under which a miniature statuette of a saint is placed.

In the convent silver eating utensils are also still preserved. There is an impressive collection of goblets. The oldest example is *the show-goblet* which was made by Jacques De Cantere Jr. in 1619 for sister Elizabeth Rouffelet, mother superior from 1616 to 1630. The remaining goblets, which bear the figure of a saint engraved from a print or a motto, are still used daily at table. Copper and bronze were also well represented. The copper was purchased from the local coppersmiths, often in return for the surrender of the old copper. Orders from bell-founders, who also made mortars and objects in brass, were sometimes placed in specialized centres such as Malines or Antwerp. There are no copper household utensils to be seen in the museum. The well-known 16th century Brugean brass-founder Jacob de Keyser made a copper *baluster-screen* for the church. This now separates the church from the Cornelius chapel. On one of the bases appear the master's marks, the craft and the city, unusual examples of coppermarks.

Horn relic of St. Cornelius.
Bruges, 16th century.
Ivory, silver, h 17.
Both ends contain relics of Cornelius and Gislenus.
A statuette of the pope crowns the centre.
Inv. O.SJ819.X

A magnificent *copper candle-crown* with twelve arms, placed in two rows, can also be seen here. The arms consist of stylized vine-tendrils which end in the candle-holders. The shaft is crowned with a madonna in an aureole. These are all stylistic elements which belong to the late gothic. Apart from some copper wall-arms and candlesticks the hospital also possesses a number of *mortars* which were made at different periods (16th, 17th, 18th centuries). They are all dated and bear the names of well-known brass-founders.

Although the dinner things used in the sick-wards were mainly made of pewter, there is little to say about them. The majority was sold or given away at the beginning of this century, when faience and lacquered utensils replaced the pewter. It is now largely to be found in private collections. Dishes, plates, tankards, bowls, cups and spoons were bought from Brugean pewtersmiths. On these objects in addition to their stamps the house-mark of St. John's was also struck : the lamb and the chalice. The small amount of pewter which has survived is now to be seen in the pharmacy. It concerns *the lids* of the pharmacists' pots which were supplied in the 18th and 19th centuries by among others François D'Hollander (18th century) and the Vande Casteele family (19th century).

Mortar.
Bruges, Joachim Blanpain, 1644.
Bronze, h 33.5.
Inv. O.SJ67.XI

Mortar.
Malines, Jan Van den Ghein II, 1568.
Bronze, h 21.5.
Inv. O.SJ68.XI

Mortar.
Bruges, Marc Le Serre, 1582.
Bronze, h 14.5, d 17.7.
Inv. O.SJ69.XI

Candle-crown.
Flanders, beginning 16th century.
Copper, h 93.5.
Inv. O.SJ765.XI

Pottery and glass

HOUSEHOLD EFFECTS IN POTTERY HAVE not been preserved. Once again it is from the accounts that we find that large quantities of pots, pans and jugs were ordered. But these fragile objects did not survive long.

The *glazed pottery of the pharmacy* has on the other hand been largely preserved. About twenty jugs, a couple of small casks and a case-bottle in brown glazed grès probably form part of the orders mentioned between 1643 and 1645 when the premises were established. They originate from Bouffioulx, an important production centre for this type of pottery in the 16th and 17th centuries. They are decorated with profile frames, stamps, motifs in relief and coats-of-arms. These last, used as property marks by the person who originally ordered them, were later repeatedly used purely as a decorative element. Some examples owe their name to the decoration which appears on the neck, these being the bearded jugs.

Page 118.
Bearded jug.
Bouffioulx, first half 17th century.
Stoneware, h 46. Coat-of-arms of Leonard Houwen.
Inv. O.SJ498.XXI

Jug.
Bouffioulx, second quarter 17th century.
Grey stoneware, h. 32.5.
Arms of Leonard Colchon, abbot in 1625 in Seligenstadt.
Inv. O.SJ502.XXI

Field bottle.
Bouffioulx, mid 17th century.
Stoneware, h 47. Inv. O.SJ497.XXI

Barrel jug.
Bouffioulx, mid 17th century.
Stoneware, h 34.4.
Arms of Fernandez de San Vittores and of Horion.
Inv. O.SJ72.XXI

About fifty recipients in white glazed pottery, the so-called *Delft pottery*, have a 17th century design. It is difficult, however to date this series or to establish the identity of the potter since all marks are lacking. It is well known that Delft was an important production centre for this type of pottery, but work of this kind was also imitated elsewhere, usually anonymously. There are various types : bottles, cylindrical pots with or without nozzles and syrup pots on legs. Typical for Delft is the blue cartouche with peacock motif, angels' heads and skulls, in which the Latin name of the medicine contained in it is painted.

Pottery, and *tiles* in particular, were frequently used for lining walls. They are to be found in the convent, in the sacristy and in the pharmacy with adjoining drawing-room. Under the window in the guardians' room a whole series of so-called Delft tiles with children's games is to be seen. They date from the end of the 17th century, for in 1694 a large number of 'tiles of children's games' was purchased from a wholesale merchant named François Brecht.

Three pharmacist's pots *after 17th century Delft models. Faience.*
Inv. O.SJ453.XXI (h 18.8)
Inv. O.SJ439.XXI (h 16.5)
Inv. O.SJ466.XXI (h 26.5)

Page 121.
Delft tiles with children's games,
17th century.
These tiles are to be seen in the guardians' room.

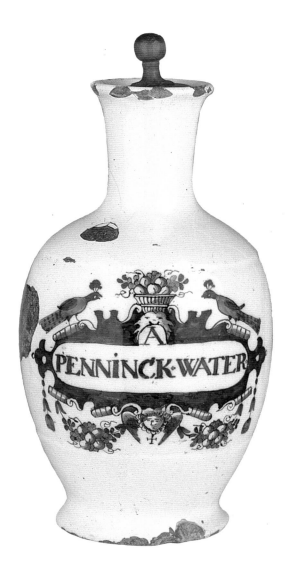

The majority of glass items which have been preserved is of fairly recent date. Among these are a series of 19th century and even 20th century *pharmacists' bottles* with glass domes. The oldest are provided with a gilded label.

Some *window-medallions*, whose origin has not yet been accounted for, date from 1538. They are rare survivals of 16th century stained glass.

An unusual item on account of its link with Brugean hospital history and its artistic value is the so-called *Friendship Cup*. This glass beaker was made in 1664. The metal mounts consist of gilded silver. Six medallions are engraved on the side of the cup : the coat-of-arms of Bruges, the b of Bruges, the coat-of-arms of the St. John's Hospital, of the Magdalen Hospice, of St. Julian's and of the Potterie. Above is the text : 'Eendraecht Mackt Maecht'. According to tradition, at the appointment of a new superior the toast was drunk from this cup.

Friendship cup, 1664.
Glass, h 22. Inv. O.SJ297.XXII

Pharmacist's bottle.
Glass, 19th century. Inv. O.SJ547.XXII

Glass medallions with the lamentation and the crucifixion, 1538.
Inv. O.SJ79 a-b.XXII (⌀ 30 and 29)

Ground-plan church
St. John's Hospital
(Memlingmuseum)

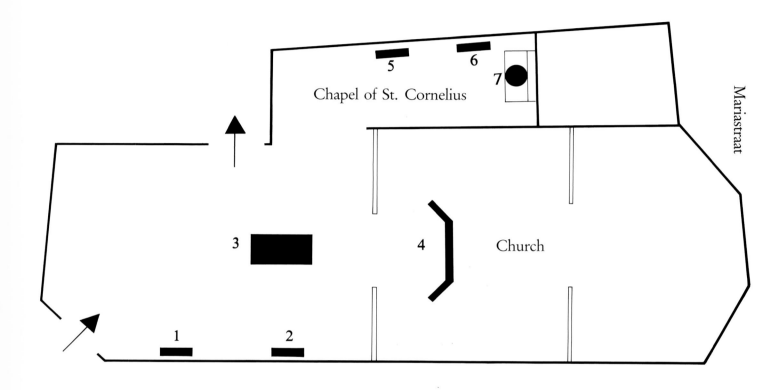

Mariastraat

Chapel of St. Cornelius

5

6

7

3

4

Church

1

2

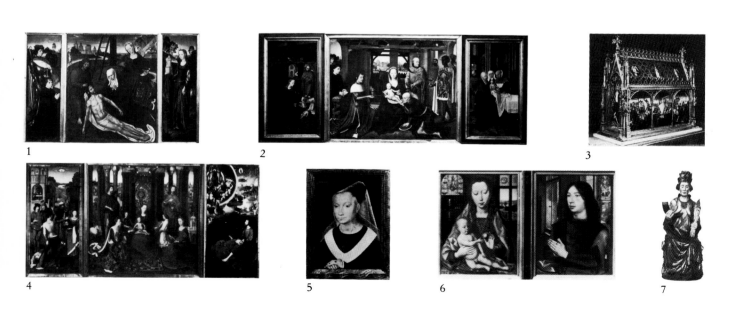

1

2

3

4

5

6

7

Ground-plan
St. John's Hospital

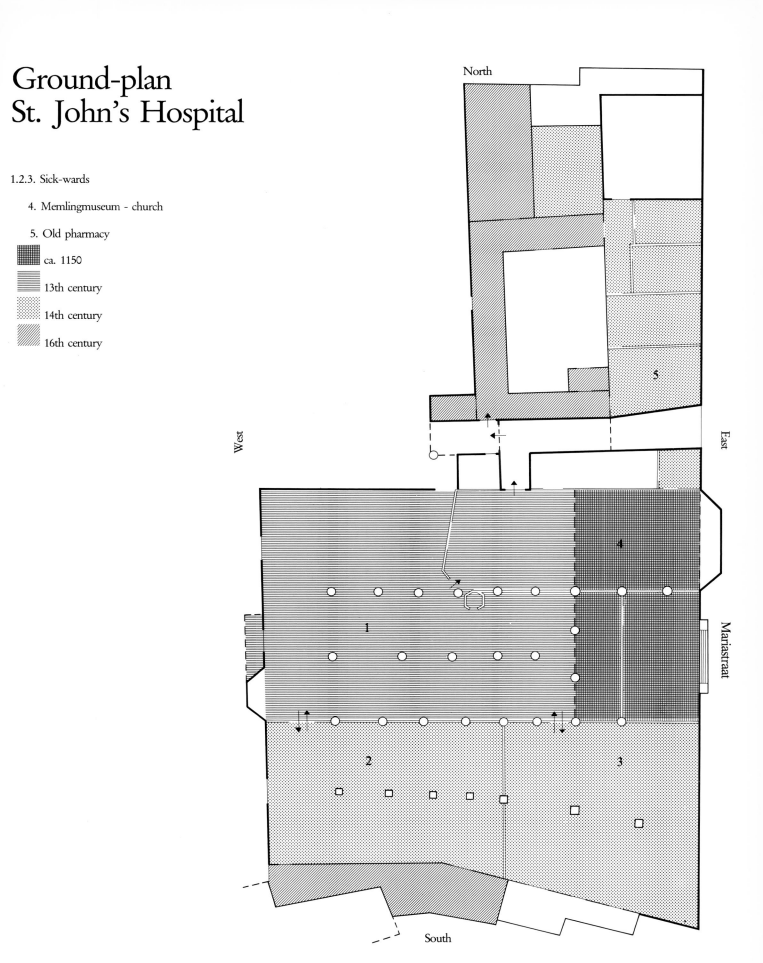

1.2.3. Sick-wards

4. Memlingmuseum - church

5. Old pharmacy

ca. 1150

13th century

14th century

16th century

North

West

East

Mariastraat

South

© LUDION S.A. - CULTURA NOSTRA - Brussels 1987

Photography : H. Maertens

Book design : J. Van Damme

Press : Die Keure Bruges

Translation : M. Cumberlege

D/4907/1987/8

Hans Memling (1435/50 - 1494).
Detail of right-hand panel of the altarpiece of St. John the Baptist and St. John the Evangelist, 1479.

Last page.
Lock-plate and handle on a 15th century oak door. It locks the archive room in the tower.

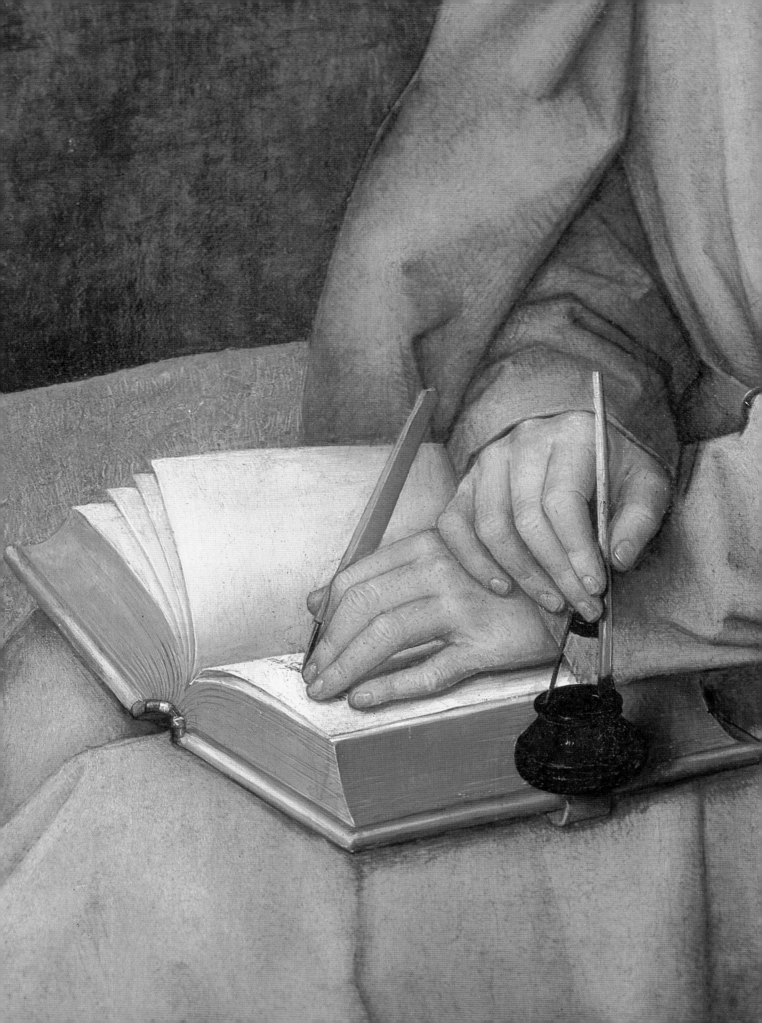